MILNER CRAFT SERIES

DECORATED EGGS

RUBY M. BROWN

SALLY MILNER PUBLISHING

DEDICATION

This book is dedicated to my husband and two daughters. Without their continuing support for my work, I would not be able to continue my writing program.

ACKNOWLEDGEMENTS

I wish to express my most sincere thanks and appreciation to my family and others who have made many contributions to the publication of this book:

To my precious husband Kevin, for all the time, love and understanding you have expressed in our home while this book was being written. Without your untiring support for my work as an author, it would never have been possible.

To my two daughters, Maria and Angela-Mary, to whom I am devoted. Your continued interest in my work as an author is very much appreciated.

To the contributing artists; Dawn Bisceglie, Joan Carey, Maureen Collins, Kate Coombe, Sandra Grieves, Ros Gunn, Val Lade, John Lindsay, Alison Nicholls, Robyn Purcell, Susan Roach, Vicki Roberts, Marice Sariola, Jan and Jenny Weatherstone.

To the contributing sketch artists; Jan and Jenny Weatherstone and Robbie Winterflood for their work with sketches.

To the photographer Benjamin Wrigley for his spectacular photography.

To Sally Milner and the staff of Sally Milner Publishing for their continuing support of my work as one of their authors.

First published in 1997 by
Sally Milner Publishing Pty Ltd
at The Pines'
RMB 54 Burra Road
Burra Creek NSW 2620 Australia

© Copyright, Ruby Brown, 1997

Design by Anna Warren
Photography by Ben Wrigley
Illustrated by Robin Winterflood
Printed and bound in Hong Kong

National Library of Australia Cataloguing-in-Publication data:

Brown, Ruby
    Decorated Eggs

    ISBN 1 86351 181 4

    1. Egg decoration. I. Title (Series: Milner Craft Series).

    745.5944

CONTENTS

INTRODUCTION

In pre-Christian times decorated eggs were known among the Chinese, Egyptians, and Persians. During the fourth century A.D., a decorated egg was found in a Romano-Germanic sarcophagus near Worms in Germany. In Persia, The Feast of the New Year was known as the Feast of the Red Egg.

Red was the most popular colour for decorated eggs up until the Middle Ages. Today, in some countries, red eggs are associated with Easter. In Hungary the 'red egg' and the 'Easter egg' are known by the same word 'kokonya'. An old Rumanian saying is 'If Christians ever stop dyeing Easter eggs red, the end of the world is at hand'. Maundy Thursday in Greece is known as 'Red Thursday'. This is the day when eggs are dyed. Red eggs are regarded as genuine Easter eggs with other colours added only for modern day variety. Red symbolises the colour of fire, of love, loyalty and of course the colour of the blood that was shed on Good Friday.

In Australia red eggs have not had a prominent place at Easter time. Our varied collection of Easter eggs is supposed to be symbolic of new life and the resurrection. Unfortunately this is not publicised by those who market Easter eggs for a substantial profit.

Eggs can be decorated and given for gifts at Easter time. Easter is a time to share eggs. When an egg is decorated before it is given it has a brightness that adds to the gift.

PREPARATION OF EGGS

Hard-boiled eggs are the easiest to use for dyeing and decorating, but they will not keep indefinitely.

1. Place the required number of eggs into a large saucepan and cover with cold water.

2. Bring to the boil. It is important that the eggs are brought slowly to the boil so the shells do not crack.

3. Allow eggs to simmer for 15 minutes.

4. Carefully remove eggs from water and allow eggs to cool and dry completely before further use.

BLOWN EGGS

Some egg decorators prefer to work on an egg that has had the contents removed. This is known as a 'blown' egg. Artists who have spent a lot of time working on an egg may want it to keep indefinitely. Blown eggs may be kept a long time if they are completely clean and dry on the inside, and are handled with care.

Blowing an Egg

For best results, eggs must be at room temperature. It is advisable to use eggs that are one to two weeks old as the egg white in fresh eggs is more difficult to remove. If you use eggs that are a few weeks old, the job of blowing an egg is made a little easier.

1. Make a hole in each end of the egg by pushing a darning needle through the shell. The fatter end of the egg becomes the bottom and the hole at this end must be enlarged. Do this by chipping the tiniest piece of shell away with the point of the needle. The secret is to do this a little at a time. If you attempt to remove too large a piece at one time, the shell will crack. The size of this hole needs to be just large enough for the blunt end of a wooden food skewer to be inserted.

2. Once the hole is the correct size, insert the darning needle gently into the egg and twist it around to break up the yolk. It is necessary to break up the yolk so it can be pushed out of the shell. Blow into the smaller hole on top of egg. Continue to blow gently until all the egg is removed from inside the shell. The contents of the egg can be saved for other uses as desired.

3. When the egg is completely emptied, cover the small hole with your finger and hold the large hole under gently running

cold water. When there is approximately a couple of table-spoons of water inside the shell, cover the large hole with another finger and give a thor-ough shake. Blow out well. Repeat.

4. Scrub outer shell of egg with a light scouring powder to remove any marks and grease spots.

5. Prop egg upright on some crum-pled tissues. Angle it slightly with the large hole at the bot-tom and allow to drain and dry thoroughly for a few days. It is important for all the moisture to be dried. The egg shell is very porous and water must not be trapped inside.

Hanging blown eggs
Eggs can be hung with a match-stick, bead or ribbon bow. See dia-grams below.

Holding blown eggs
Carefully poke a thin knitting nee-dle or skewer through the holes that were used to blow the egg. Work can easily be done on the egg supporting it with the needle. The needle can be secured at both ends to allow the egg to dry. When completely dry remove nee-dle from egg.

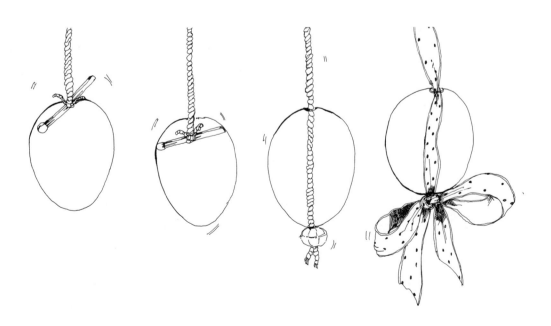

Artists' Eggs

BREAD DOUGH DESIGN EGGS

DESIGNED AND MADE BY SUSAN ROACH

Artistic work using bread dough has been practised for many centuries. During the depression years when there was little money available for 'extras', people made jewellery using bread dough. The art of working with bread dough has progressed from jewellery making and is now applied to a wide variety of crafts.

Bread Dough Design Egg 1

MATERIALS

3 slices white bread (Use sliced white bread that is a few days old, as it is easier to crumb.)

Electric blender

Old ice cream container

P V A glue (Selley's Aquadhere is suitable)

Iceblock sticks (These are easy to stir with and they can be thrown away after use.)

Acrylic paints: white, pink, mauve, green, blue, beige. (Matisse acrylic paints are economical and have a wide range of colours. They are available from art suppliers.)

1 egg

Darning needle

Artist's paint brush (These are available from art suppliers.)

Satin water-based varnish. (This can be obtained from hardware stores.)

Small sharp scissors

Large and small 'Forget-Me-Not' Ejector Cutters (These are available from specialist cake decorating shops.)

Berri pins (These are available from specialist haberdashery shops.)

Stitch unpicker (Break off metal point leaving ball shape. The rounded ball end is used for pressing the small dough balls into the centre of flowers while the reverse end is used to shape the actual flowers.)

Smooth laminated board

Plastic rolling pin (A 20cm, 8", long piece of P V C piping can be used if a plastic rolling pin is not available.)

Stamens (These are available from specialist cake decorating shops.)

Preparing the dough

1. Remove all the crusts from the 3 slices bread.

2. Crumb the bread using an electric blender.

3. Place crumbs into an ice cream container.

4. Add 30 ml (1 tablespoon) of Aquadhere and mix with an ice-block stick until the glue has been dispersed evenly with the crumbs.

5. This next step is messy but it is a very important part of the finished product: Take a handful of dough and knead it with your hands. The dough will be sticky to start with, but will soften and become smoother as you knead. The dough is ready when it is very smooth and soft with no lumps. Always cover the dough with plastic wrap to prevent a dry crust forming and keep it supple. Use the dough within 10 days.

6. Blend the soft dough with white acrylic paint to give it a solid base consistency to which any other colour can be added later.

About 1 teaspoon of white paint should be sufficient. Knead the paint into the dough to give a very white appearance. The dough is now ready for other colours to be added.

7. Break dough into 5 portions. Reserve one portion. Colour some dough pink for the roses and mauve for the large Forget-Me-Nots. Colour a little dough green for the leaves and some blue for the centres of the small white Forget-Me-Nots. The colours are kneaded in, starting with a small 'dob' of coloured paint only — you can always add more later — until you get the colour you desire.

Preparing the egg

1. Blow the egg following the instructions given on page 5.

2. Using a paint brush, paint the egg a beige shade giving two coats. Allow to dry between coats. When the paint has dried, varnish with satin water-based varnish for prolonged protection. Allow to dry.

Caring for brushes

Wash brushes with soap and water and rinse well. Brushes will be preserved by coating with soap after use and allowing to dry. Rinse brushes well before using again. Try to avoid damaging brushes; never leave the point of a brush sitting in water.

Adding decorations

You will need 1 rose, 4 double buds, 4 single buds, 4 large Forget-Me-Nots, 12 small Forget-Me-Nots and 11 leaves for this project.

Making the rose

1. From the pink dough, take a small piece of dough approximately the size of a marble and make a ball. Press one side of the ball flat. Lay the flat side across your thumb and roll inwards with the other hand to form the bud. Form a petal by following the same procedure, but do not roll inward. Instead roll the petal around the bud. Add a little white to pink dough. Continue making petals, overlapping them progressively until 5 petals have been positioned around the bud.

2. After placing the petals around the bud, squeeze the dough gently between your fingers to shape the base of the rose.

3. Cut off the excess dough with small sharp scissors.

Making double and single buds

To make a single bud: Take a small piece of green dough approximately the size of a marble. Shape into a ball. Press one side of the ball flat. Lay the flat side across your thumb and roll inwards with the other hand to form the bud.

To make a double bud: A double bud is formed by adding one petal to a single bud.

Flowers and leaves

The smaller flowers shown on the egg are made using a metal ejector cutter.

1. Place a small piece of mauve dough onto laminated board.

2. Roll dough out to 2 mm (1/10") thickness.

3. Using a large Forget-Me-Not flower-shape, press ejector cutter into dough. Lift and push on spring loaded pin to release flower. Make 4 large Forget-Me-Not flowers. Using a smaller shape make 12 small Forget-Me-Nots from white dough.

4. Make 11 leaves, by moulding some green dough into a small cone shape. Indent into the dough a vein, marked with a Berri pin.

Assembling the decoration on the egg

1. To steady the egg while you decorate it, place a little dough at the bottom of the egg.

2. Glue rose at top of egg. Add double buds evenly around egg, gluing into rose. Glue single buds under each double bud, using the ball end of a Berri pin.

3. Mould 4 small Forget-Me-Nots using the ball end of a Berri pin and glue into buds, followed by leaves as shown in diagram.

4. Using rounded end of stitch unpicker, mould 4 large mauve Forget-Me-Nots. Glue these shapes between the double buds

pushing gently into rose. Cut 8 stamens to 10 mm (⅜") in length and glue 2 into centre of each mauve Forget-Me-Not. Mould remaining 8 small white Forget-Me-Nots with the ball end of a Berri pin. Gently push 2 white flowers under each mauve Forget-Me-Not.

5. Finish using the remaining leaves. Glue one under each mauve Forget-Me-Not and 3 around the top of the egg.

6. Form small balls of blue dough. Glue into centre of each small white Forget-Me-Not, using the ball end of stitch unpicker.

Drying dough

Place finished egg onto an elevated wire rack. The elevated rack allows air to circulate under the finished work, ensuring work dries evenly. Place rack in a warm, well ventilated area to facilitate drying process. The work will take 2-3 days to dry. It is important to allow the finished product to dry naturally. It will shrink to about 75 per cent of its original size when it is completely dry. When dough is completely dry, varnish all over the flowers.

Bread Dough Design Egg II

MATERIALS

3 slices white bread (use sliced white bread that is a few days old, as it is easier to crumb)

Electric blender

Old ice cream container

P V A glue (Selley's Aquadhere is suitable)

Iceblock sticks (These are easy to stir with and they can be thrown away after use.)

Acrylic paints: apricot, grey, white, lemon, green, blue, beige and dark peach. (Matisse acrylic paints are economical and have a wide range of colours. They are available from art suppliers.)

1 egg

Darning needle

Artist's paint brush (These are available from art suppliers.)

Satin water-based varnish (This can be obtained from hardware stores.)

Sea-sponge

Small sharp scissors

6-petal, pointed, flower-shaped aluminium cutter

Large and small Forget-Me-Not Ejector Cutters (These are available from specialist cake decorating shops.)

Berri pins (These are available from specialist haberdashery shops.)

Stitch unpicker (Break off metal point leaving ball shape. The rounded ball end is used for pressing the small dough balls into the centre of flowers while the reverse end is used to shape the actual flowers.)

Smooth laminated board

Plastic rolling pin (A 20 cm, 8", long piece of PVC piping can be used if a plastic rolling pin is not available.)

Stamens (These are available from specialist cake decorating shops.)

Preparing the dough

1. Follow steps 1 – 6 on page 8.
7. Break dough into 6 portions. Reserve one portion. Colour some dough apricot for the roses, grey for the pointed flower shape and lemon for the small Forget-Me-Nots. Colour a little dough green for the leaves and some blue for the centres of the lemon Forget-Me-Nots. Colours can be kneaded into the dough. Start with a small 'dob' of coloured paint — you can always add more later — until you get the colour you desire.

Preparing the egg

1. Blow the egg following the instructions given on page 5.
2. Using a paint brush, paint the egg a beige shade giving two coats. Allow to dry between coats. When the paint has dried varnish with satin water-based varnish for prolonged protection. Allow to dry.
3. Using some dark peach shade, and a sea sponge, dab paint all over the egg. Allow paint to dry.

Caring for brushes
(See page 8)

REQUIREMENTS
You will need 1 rose, 2 double buds, 2 single buds, 2 six pointed grey flowers, 2 large white Forget-Me-Nots, 6 small lemon Forget-Me-Nots and 10 leaves for this project.

Making the roses
Using the apricot dough, follow the steps to make a rose described on page 9.

Double and single buds
Using the apricot dough follow the instructions for making single and double buds described on page 9.

Flowers and leaves
The smaller flowers shown on the egg are made using a metal ejector cutter.

1. Place a small piece of grey dough onto laminated board. Roll out to 2 mm ($\frac{1}{10}$") thickness.
2. Press a 6 petal pointed flower-shape aluminium cutter into dough. Remove dough from cutter and mould flower with the end of a stitch unpicker. Cut 2 grey flowers.
3. Roll out some white dough to about 2 mm ($\frac{1}{10}$") thickness.

Using a large Forget-Me-Not flower-shape, press ejector cutter into dough. Lift and push on spring loaded pin to release flower. Make 2 large white For-get-Me-Not flowers.

4. Roll out some lemon dough. Using a smaller shape make 6 small Forget-Me-Nots.

5. Make 10 leaves, by moulding some green dough into a small cone shape. Indent into the dough a vein, marked with a Berri pin.

Assembling the decoration on the egg

1. To steady the egg while you decorate it, place a little dough at the bottom of the egg.

2. Following diagram on page 10, glue rose in middle of egg. Glue double buds on each side of rose at a slight angle across the egg. Next to the double buds, glue the single buds, and each side of the single buds, the grey flowers. Gently push buds into sides of the rose.

3. On the opposite sides of the rose add the large white Forget-Me-Nots. Glue the 6 small lemon Forget-Me-Nots evenly around the rose.

4. Glue leaves around flowers.

5. Form small balls of blue dough. Glue into centre of each small white Forget-Me-Not, using the ball end of stitch unpicker.

6. Cut 4 stamens to 10 mm ($\frac{3}{8}$") in length and glue 2 into each grey flower.

Drying dough

Follow instructions given on page 10.

PAPER TOLE

DESIGNED AND MADE BY JENNY WEATHERSTONE AND MAUREEN COLLINS

Working with paper has seen the revival of many ancient forms of craft such as découpage, paper making, and papier maché. Paper tole is a derivation of découpage, being known as a three-dimensional découpage technique. Identical prints are cut out and layered with silicone glue between each layer to create a three-dimensional picture. Skill is necessary to gently shape, curve or position cut-out paper pieces at an angle to create realism in the picture. Each layer must be carefully built up to give a third dimension to particular sections of the picture. Intricate works of art are lacquered for lasting protection.

Blue Bell Baby
REQUIREMENTS

1 blown egg

May Gibbs bush babies wrapping paper (blue bell babies) (Available at newsagents and craft outlets.)

fine pointed craft scissors and/or craft knife

cutting boards

Selley's silicone roof and gutter sealant

Bostik glue stick

tweezers

METHOD
STEP 1

Cut out baby sitting amongst flowers and extra foliage if desired. Glue to egg using glue stick.

STEP 2

To create the 3-dimensional effect of the picture, cut out the baby's front leg, arms and bonnet in one piece (as shown in diagram).

Place round dobs of silicone all over the underside of the piece. Using tweezers, carefully place the piece over the corresponding part of the first layer. Make sure not to press it down as it should sit approx. 4 mm ($\frac{3}{16}$") above the first layer.

STEP 3

Cut out petals from bonnet (shown in diagram). Run the glue stick along the back of the petals on the bottom edge. Place small dobs of silicone under top of petals. Using tweezers, place the piece over the petals on the second layer and gently press the bottom edge down so that it sits nicely on the face.

STEP 4

To finish off, cut out a flower and place over the hole in the top of the egg.

Cut out some foliage and glue it down so that it looks like it is hanging. Glue a lady bug on the end of the foliage so that it appears that the baby is looking at it.

Wattle Babies

REQUIREMENTS

1 blown egg

May Gibbs bush babies wrapping paper (blue bell babies) (Available at Newsagents and Craft outlets.)

fine pointed craft scissors and/or craft knife

cutting boards

Selley's silicone roof and gutter sealant

Bostik glue stick

METHOD

STEP 1

Cut out 2 leaves for each baby to sit on. Cut out 2 wattle babies. Glue the leaves and babies to the egg using the glue stick.

STEP 2

To make the picture 3-dimensional, cut out (from the baby on the left) the front arm and leg as one piece. Cut the bonnet separately. Refer to diagram.

Place dobs of silicone on the underside of the pieces. Using tweezers, place the pieces over the corresponding parts of the first paper. Do not press them down as they should sit up approx. 4 mm (³⁄₁₆") above the first layer.

STEP 3

To make the baby on the right into a 3-dimensional figure, cut out the piece as shown in diagram.

Repeat the procedure with the silicone as shown in Step 2.

STEP 4

To finish off, cut out a gum nut from the May Gibbs Gum Blossom Babies wrapping paper and glue over the hole in the top of the egg.

Rabbit on Stump

REQUIREMENTS

1 blown egg

wrapping paper (with rabbit motif) (Available at Newsagents and Craft outlets.)

fine pointed craft scissors and/or craft knife

cutting boards

Selley's silicone roof and gutter sealant

Bostik glue stick

tweezers

METHOD

STEP 1

Cut out rabbit, stump and foliage. Glue to egg using glue stick.

STEP 2

To create the 3-dimensional effect of the picture, cut out the stump and rabbit again as one piece (as shown in diagram).

Place round dobs of silicone all over the underside of the piece. Using tweezers, carefully place the piece over the corresponding part of the first layer. Make sure not to press it down as it should sit approx. 4 mm (³⁄₁₆") above the first layer.

STEP 3

Cut out rabbit (shown in diagram). Place small dobs of silicone on the under side of rabbit. Using tweezers, place over the existing rabbit on the second layer.

STEP 4

To finish off, cut out the foliage (as shown in diagram) at the base of the stump. Place small dobs of silicone on the underside and using tweezers position over corresponding foliage on base of stump.

ICON EGGS

On a recent visit to Western Australia I had the pleasure of meeting one of Australia's leading artists, Marice Sariola, in her Icon Studio. I have included her work here because it is so wonderful and is part of the tradition of egg decorating. I have not attempted to give full details on how to paint these eggs as it does require specialist skills. However, diagrams of the paintings are included and they will help you to create a version of these eggs yourself.

Marice Sariola was born in Finland and spent 10 years of her life in Sweden. When she arrived in Australia in 1989 she brought with her an international reputation in iconography, which is the art of creating icons.

The versatility of Marice's work is shown here. Her art takes many forms and painting eggs is one of her great loves as she explains :

'There are several legends about the origin of egg painting. One tells how Mary from Magdala, after Christ's Resurrection, travelled to Rome to meet Emperor Tiberian. She gave the Emperor a red painted egg saying: "Christ is risen". Mary also spread word about the Crucifixion.

'Mary's egg became the very first Easter egg and the tradition of giving eggs spread among Christians, who see the egg as a symbol for the Resurrection and the New Life.

'There is another legend about Mary from Magdala. This tells that Mary had a basket of eggs with her at Calvary, when Jesus was Crucified. Blood from the Cross ran down to the basket and formed certain patterns on the eggs. Eggs painted with these red patterns are still, today, customary Easter gifts in some East European countries.

'Mary from Magdala however, did not invent the tradition of giving eggs. The tradition was widespread among the Jews. Poorer people, especially, used to give eggs to friends and to hosts on their birthdays and also in the New Year. Later, multicoloured eggs replaced red ones. Bible verses, pictures of churches and icons were painted on them.

'At Easter, the Orthodox Church places eggs on the Altar, or they are hung beneath an icon.

'This tradition is today spreading into Western Churches as well.

PAPER TOLE EGGS

ICON EGGS

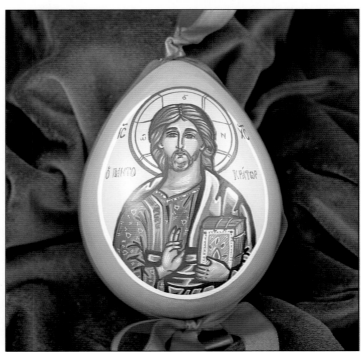

TOP: QUILLING. LEFT, BASKET OF FLOWERS, CENTRE, WILD FLOWERS OF AUSTRALIA, RIGHT, TEARDROPS

RIGHT: QUILLED CHRISTMAS EGG

BELOW: SPRING FLOWERS

Above: Etching

Below: Elegant Eggs: top left, duck egg with rhinestones on swan stand; top centre, duck egg with angel figurine; top right, goose egg with pink base, cut-out lid with pearls and gold rose; bottom left, duck egg with gold findings and pearls; Bottom right; duck egg with heart-shaped dome.

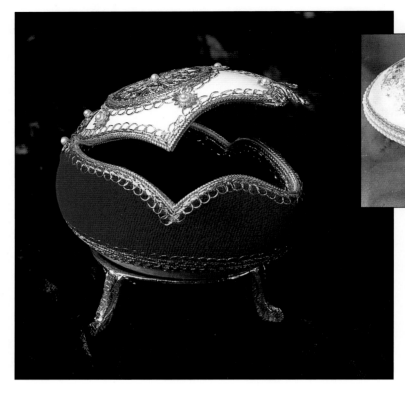

ABOVE: GOOSE EGG
WITH OLD ENGLISH
DECAL

ABOVE: ELEGANT EGG:
GOOSE EGG WITH RED
VELVET BASE, WHITE TOP
AND GOLD DOME INSET

RIGHT: DÉCOUPAGE

BELOW: YELLOW CHICK IN
DECORATED EGG SHELL

TOP: FOLK ART. LEFT, LARGE COTTAGE GARDEN EGG, CENTRE, BERRY EGG, RIGHT, GRAPE EGG.
INSET: WARATAH EGG

ABOVE LEFT: ICING FLOWERS

ABOVE RIGHT: ICING AND DRIED FLOWERS

RIGHT: ONION SKIN DYED EGGS

BASKET OF EGGS INCLUDING: 1. EASTER CHICK; 2. HAND-PAINTED COUNTRY SCENE; 3. HAND-PAINTED BLUE BACKGROUND WITH WHITE FLOWERS; 4. WAX MARBLING; 5. DRIED FLOWERS; 6. LEAF PRINTS; 7. GOLD LEAVES, BRAID AND BEADS; 8. SILVER BRAID AND GLITTER; 9. DRIED FLOWERS AND GREEN RIBBON BOW; 10. WAXING; 11. PAPER CUT-OUTS; 12. HAND-PAINTED FLOWERS; 13. RED PAINT WITH GOLD PAINT SPLATTERS; 14. DRIED LAQUERED FLOWERS; 15. BEADS; 16. TRANSFERS OF SMALL BIRDS AND BUTTERFLIES. (SEE DIAGRAM)

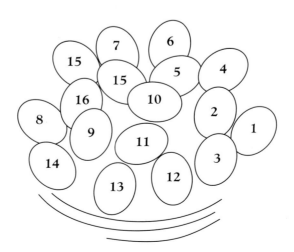

The eggs shown in this book were commissioned for the Diocese of Linkoping, The Church of Sweden.

'There are two choices of material for icon eggs. These are genuine hen or goose eggs or wooden eggs. Bird eggs can be painted directly, but I prefer eggs of solid wood as they are less fragile and offer a chance of using the traditional icon technique.

'Wooden eggs are coated with rabbit skin glue and gesso, a mixture of this glue and chalk powder.

'The paint is of traditional egg tempera, mineral pigments, water and egg yolk, which is used as a binding medium. This paint does not fade with time and is the only worthy material to the tradition, where Holy Images and Christian symbols are painted.'

QUILLING

DESIGNED AND MADE BY JENNY WEATHERSTONE,
ROBYN PURCELL AND JAN WEATHERSTONE

Paper quilling is based on the same principles as the gold and silver filigree art of the silversmiths. This technique has been practised for many centuries and uses rolled strips of silver and gold. It is thought that the technique has been used with paper since the Chinese invented that product in 105 AD. The art of curling paper around a quill gave the craft its name.

In Europe evidence of paper quilling appeared in churches around the twelfth century when it was used as religious decoration. In the Victorian era the art of quilling became very fashionable with the ladies of the time and there are examples of early quilling exhibited in museums. Unfortunately, a lot of original paper quilling has been lost over the years.

Today the craft is practised in England, France, the United States and many other countries. In recent times it has gained popularity in Australia with people making greeting cards, decorated boxes, jewellery, decorative art work and decorated eggs.

REQUIREMENTS
1 blown egg
acrylic paint (apply 2 coats to eggs making sure to wait for each coat to dry before applying quilled flowers)
paper strips (available from specialist craft suppliers)
quilling tool (a needle tool will give best effect with fine paper
craft glue (PVA was used as this dries clear)
tooth pick (used to apply glue)
fine tweezers (to position flowers)

GENERAL TECHNIQUES
This is a brief description of some of the shapes you can make with your paper. Remember to practise many times before you work a piece you wish to keep.

TIGHT ROLL
Insert paper into tool and turn the tool, rolling up all the paper. Glue while still on the tool, holding in place tightly.

TEARDROP
Insert paper into tool and turn the

tool, rolling up all the paper. Relax the rolled paper and secure with glue to form a loose roll. Then pinch one end of the loose circle.

MARQUISE SHAPE

Make a loose roll, as above, then pinch at two points on opposite sides. This is sometimes called an eye shape.

LEAF SHAPE

Make as for marquise shape above, then curve points in opposite direction. (Or, you can cut various lengths of paper in the shape of leaves, using curved scissors.)

MOON SHAPE

Make a loose roll, as above, then curve around thumb tip. Pinch the ends.

FRINGED TIGHT ROLL

First fringe the length of paper required. Using the same technique as the tight roll glue while still on the tool, holding tightly. Do not take off the tool at this stage - just gently feather out the fringed side of the paper to form the blossom look.

SCROLLS

These are made to various shapes — see diagrams in the projects. Cut off the required length of paper. Wind on the tool from each end from whichever side is required.

Wild Flowers of Australia

METHOD
Wattle Flowers

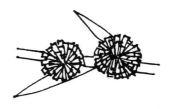

BLOSSOMS
3 mm x 5 cm (⅛" x 2")
yellow paper

STEMS
1.5 mm (1/16")
buttermilk paper
various lengths

LEAVES
1.5 mm (1/16")
buttermilk paper
make leaf shapes

Form fringed tight rolls with yellow paper for blossoms. Find and mark centre of egg and draw a fine line to position stems (buttermilk). Position wattle flowers on either side to form a border. Place leaves randomly between wattle blossoms.

FLANNEL FLOWER

PETALS
1.5 mm x 5 cm (¹⁄₁₆" x 2")
white paper
1.5 mm x 5 cm (¹⁄₁₆" x 2")
sage green paper

CENTRE
3 mm x 3.5 cm (¹⁄₈" x 1 ²⁄₅")
sage green paper

Join white to sage green approx. 3 mm (¹⁄₈") from beginning. Starting with white in tool, make 7 teardrops for each flower. Make one tight fringed roll for each flower. Arrange teardrops around each centre to form flannel flower.

STEMS
1.5 mm (¹⁄₁₆")
sage green paper
Cut strips, curve slightly and glue in place.

LEAVES
3 mm (¹⁄₈")
sage green paper
Cut into leaf shapes and place along stem of each flower.

STURTS DESERT PEA

1.5 mm x 15 cm (¹⁄₁₆" x 6")
red paper
Form 2 teardrops for each flower

CENTRES
1.5 mm x 3.5 cm (¹⁄₁₆" x 1 ²⁄₅")
black paper
Form 2 tight rolls for each flower

Use 2 large and 2 small teardrops for each flower.

Place 2 tight black rolls in centre where teardrops join each other.

STEMS
1.5 mm (¹⁄₁₆")
sage green paper
Curve and glue in place

LEAVES
6 mm (³⁄₁₆")
sage green paper
Cut 11-12 leaf shapes. Place these leaves randomly on stems.

Basket of Flowers

BASKET
3 strips 3 mm x 90 cm (⅛" x 36") long were plaited and wrapped around base of egg and stand. Remainder of plait was used to form handle of basket.

FRINGED FLOWERS
5 cm x 6 mm (2" x ³⁄₁₆") lengths lilac, pale pink, purple, rich pink and fuchsia paper

3 cm x 3 mm lengths (1⅕" x ⅛") magenta, pale pink, purple, rich pink and fuchsia paper

Fringe 6 mm (³⁄₁₆") length and join

to 3 cm (1 ⅕") length and form tight rolls.

FRINGED FLOWER BUDS

FLOWER
5 cm x 6 mm (2" x ³⁄₁₆") fringed purple paper

Form a tight roll and gently push down to form bud.

BUD CASING
10 cm x 3 mm (4" x ⅛") dark green paper

Form a tight roll with dark green and push centre out to form bell shape. Glue liberally inside and place flower bud inside this bell shape.

DAISIES

PETALS
7.5 cm x 1.5 cm (3" x ³⁄₅") purple, pink and rich pink paper 7 teardrops of each

CENTRES
5 cm x 1.5 mm (2" x 1/16")
rich pink, magenta and pink paper
1 tight roll for each

Place 7 teardrops around each centre to form daisy flowers.

Daisy bud

FLOWER
7.5 cm x 1.5 mm (3" x 1/16")
rich pink paper
1 teardrop

BUD CASING
10 cm x 3 mm (4" x 1/8")
dark green paper
1 tight roll

Form a tight roll with dark green. Push centre out to form bell shape. Glue liberally inside and place flower bud inside this bell shape.

STOCK FLOWERS

STEMS
3 cm x 1.5 cm (1 1/5" x 4/5")
dark green paper glued flat

FLOWERS
5 cm x 1.5 mm (2" x 1/16")
magenta paper
tight rolls
5 cm x 1.5 mm (2" x 1/16")
pink paper
tight rolls

LEAVES
7.5 cm x 1.5 mm (3" x 1/16")
dark green paper
teardrops

Glue tight rolls either side of stems and place 2 leaves at base, 1 either side.

TO FINISH
3 leaves of various sizes from 9 mm (3/8") wide paper were placed randomly amongst flowers in basket.

Spring Flowers

BORDER

1.5 mm (1/16")
sage green paper
enough to border egg

STOCK FLOWERS

1.5 mm x 5 cm (1/16" x 2")
pale pink paper
make 20 tight rolls

1.5 mm x 5 cm (¹⁄₁₆" x 2")
magenta paper
make 20 tight rolls

1.5 mm x 5 cm (¹⁄₁₆" x 2")
lilac paper
make 20 tight rolls

STEMS
1.5 mm x 3 cm (¹⁄₁₆" x 1 ¹⁄₅")
sage green paper
cut 12 lengths

LEAVES
6 mm x 1.5 cm (³⁄₁₆" x ⁴⁄₅")
sage green paper
make 12 teardrops

Place stems at even intervals either
side of border. Make tight rolls
and arrange 5 either side of these
stems. Place a leaf either side of
each group of stock flowers.

TOP FLOWER

PETALS
1.5 mm x 10 cm (¹⁄₁₆" x 4")
crimson paper

CENTRE
1.5 mm x 7.5 cm (¹⁄₁₆" x 3")
black paper

Make 8 teardrops arranged around
a centre of black tight roll.

FUCHSIA FLOWERS

PETALS
1.5 mm x 7.5 cm (¹⁄₁₆" x 3")
pale pink paper
form 2 teardrops for each flower

STAMENS
1.5 mm x 5 cm (¹⁄₁₆" x 2")
fuchsia paper
form 1 teardrop for each flower

STEM
1.5 mm (¹⁄₁₆")
sage green paper

Place 2 pale pink teardrops at an
angle with pointed ends touching.
Place 1 fuchsia teardrop for each
flower pointed end, between the 2
pale pink teardrops. Repeat down
stem of sage green paper. Make 8
fuchsia flowers, 4 for each side of
egg.

BLUEBELLS

FLOWERS
1.5 mm x 7.5 cm (¹⁄₁₆" x 3")
pale blue paper

STEMS
1.5 mm (¹⁄₁₆")
sage green paper

Make 18 flower petals (bunny ear shape — loose circle with a rounded indentation on 1 side) 9 placed along 1 side of stems.

DAFFODILS

PETALS
1.5 mm x 7.5 cm (¹⁄₁₆" x 3")
yellow paper

CENTRE
5 cm x 3 mm (2" x ¹⁄₈")
yellow paper

STEMS
1.5 mm (¹⁄₁₆")
sage green paper

Make 20 teardrops. Five teardrops for each flower arranged pointed side facing out around tight roll placed at top of each length of sage green. Two either side of egg.

CRIMSON FLOWER

STEM
1.5 mm (¹⁄₁₆")
sage green paper

BASE
1.5 mm x 7.5 cm (¹⁄₁₆" x 3")
sage green paper
shaped into a moon shape

CENTRE
1.5 mm x 7.5 cm (¹⁄₁₆" x 3")
black paper
make a loose roll

PETALS
1.5 mm x 7.5 cm (¹⁄₁₆" x 3")
crimson paper
make 5 marquise shaped petals

To finish off assorted size leaves were added to base of daffodils and crimson flowers.

BUTTERFLY
1.5 mm x 10 cm (¹⁄₁₆" x 4")
brown paper
form marquise shape for body

WINGS
1.5 mm x 5 cm (¹⁄₁₆" x 2")
blue paper
1.5 mm x 10 cm (¹⁄₁₆" x 4")
turquoise blue paper

ANTENNAE
1.5 mm x 3 cm (¹⁄₁₆" x 1 ¹⁄₅")
black paper

Join blue to turquoise and make 2 teardrops. Position for wings. Place antennae at front of body.

Teardrops

REQUIREMENTS
paint brush (flat, medium size artist brush)

blown egg

3 mm (¹⁄₈") wide quilling paper (assorted colours — own choice. Available from specialist craft suppliers)

quilling tool

tweezers (for placing shapes in position on egg)

toothpick (for applying glue to end of paper when making shapes)

PVA glue (Selleys Aquadhere is suitable)

acrylic paint (Jo Sonja's is suitable to use)

PREPARING THE EGG
Using a paint brush paint egg the colour of your choice. Allow to dry thoroughly.

ASSEMBLING THE EGG

STEP 1
Make 2 leaf shapes, using paper 16 cm (6 ½") in length. Glue to top of egg. Make 3 teardrops: — 1 large and 2 small. Glue into position. Finish by gluing 1 small tight coil to top of egg.

STEP 2
Make 3 teardrops using 20 cm (8") lengths of paper. Glue 2 shapes to egg. Glue a third shape on top of other 2. Add 1 tight roll and 4 single open coils.

STEP 3

Make 6 flower petal shapes using paper 20 cm (8") in length. Glue into position. Make a small tight roll for centre of flower. Add 3 single open scrolls.

STEP 4

Make 4 leaf shapes using paper 20 cm (8") in length. Make 1 teardrop shape. Glue 4 leaves to egg. Centre teardrop. Glue on top of other shapes. Add 1 tight roll and 3 single open coils.

STEP 5

Make 1 tight roll from a 60 cm (24") length of paper. Glue to base of egg. Make six teardrops (paper approx. 20 cm, 8", in length). Glue in a flower shape to form base for egg.

Repeat design on other side as desired.

Quilled Christmas Egg

REQUIREMENTS

1 blown egg

3 mm (⅛") wide quilling paper (red and green)

quilling tool

tweezers

toothpick

PVA glue (Selley's Aquadhere)

ASSEMBLING THE EGG

STEP 1

Make 18 teardrop shapes by rolling 6 cm (2 ⅖") lengths of green paper

around tool. Remove roll and allow it to unroll slightly to form a loose roll. To make a teardrop, pinch one end of roll between thumb and fore-finger to form a point. Using a toothpick, glue the end of the roll down to prevent unravelling.

STEP 2

Make 6 tight rolls by rolling 3 cm (1 ⅕") lengths of red paper around quilling tool. Remove from tool, being careful not to let it unroll. Glue end to secure it.

STEP 3

Arrange green tear drops and red rolls into a wreath as shown in the diagram. (Diagram is approximately actual size.) Repeat wreath on other side of egg if desired.

STEP 4

Make 2 more tight red rolls using 6 cm (2 ⅖") lengths of paper for each one, then glue. Using pointed end of quilling tool, gently push centre of each roll until a bell shape is formed. Paint inside of each bell with Aquadhere so that they maintain their shape.

STEP 5

Cut 2 thin strips of red paper and glue a bell to the end of each shape. Secure other end of strip so that bells appear to be hanging from wreath. Make 2 red loops for a bow and attach to top of wreath.

STEP 6

Make approx. 30 assorted scrolls of different shapes and sizes (as in diagram).

Paint the scrolls with Aquadhere to secure them.

Arrange scrolls in a border right around egg.

STEP 7

The base is made from:

× 1

× 4

× 4

Arrange scrolls as shown in diagram and glue together to form a base.

ETCHING

Care is necessary when working with acid when etching designs. Any acid contact with the skin should be washed off immediately to prevent burns. Weak solutions of hydrochloric acid are poisonous and so extreme care should be taken during etching.

Children should not be allowed to work with strong acids. Children can work with mild acids such as lemon juice, vinegar or sauerkraut juice. The acid in these items is in a weak form and as a result the procedure takes longer for the acid to etch into the dye.

REQUIREMENTS

Etching pen

Quills

Wooden matchstick or tooth pick (Repeated contact of acid on metal nibs will cause nibs to rust. Because of this some people prefer to work with disposable items.)

Acid (3% solution hydrochloric acid)

blown and dyed eggs (strong colours are best for a contrast)

soft absorbent cloths

salad oil (for polishing finished egg)

METHOD

1. First dye your egg to a colour of your choice. See page 68 for instructions on dyeing.

2. Carefully dip etching tool into acid. Draw a design on the surface of a dyed egg. Carefully wipe off excess acid with absorbent cloth. Work only small portions of design at a time. Acid will remove colour

wherever it contacts the dyed egg, so care is necessary when applying acid during the etching process.

3. When egg is completely decorated as desired, rinse with cool water and pat dry with a clean soft cloth.

4. Polish egg with a drop of salad oil.

See diagrams above for possible designs for etching.

ELEGANT EGGS

DESIGNED AND WORKED BY VICKI ROBERTS

Elegant eggs are not designed for the inexperienced. Accuracy and patience are two essential requirements when making these eggs. The end results can be both elegant and exquisite.

Supplies for decorating these eggs can be purchased from specialist craft suppliers.

All Elegant eggs are prepared for decorating by the following method.

REQUIREMENTS

Egg to size required

Sandpaper (wet and dry, size 400 — 7 cm, 2⅘" square)

Clean water (for sanding egg)

2 rubber bands (very small bands, size 8 is most suitable)

Wooden meat skewer (shaslik stick)

Hairdryer

Narrow-neck vase

PREPARATION

1. Blow your selected egg using the method described on page 5.
2. Wet-sand egg shell using wet and dry sandpaper. Rinse frequently with clean cold water.
3. Thoroughly rinse inside and outside of egg with clean cold water.
4. Wrap 1 size 8 rubber band around meat skewer (approximately 5 times). Push approximately ⅓ way down meat skewer.
5. Gently push the meat skewer through the 2 holes in the egg shell so that it rests against the rubber band on the skewer.
6. Firmly wrap (approximately 5 times) the other size 8 rubber band around the meat skewer.
7. Push rubber band close to egg shell, so that the egg is secured between the 2 rubber bands. The skewer should fit firmly into the egg so that the skewer and the egg will turn at the same time.
8. Using hairdryer on cool setting thoroughly dry egg shell. It is necessary to constantly turn skewer to dry shell evenly. Position skewer in a narrow-neck vase to cool after drying.

Goose Egg Jewellery Box with Red Velvet Base, White Top and Gold Dome Inset

REQUIREMENTS

Goose egg, blown and prepared

Face mask (*Warning* — It is essential to wear a mask at all times when painting and cutting egg.)

Safety glasses (*Warning* — It is essential to wear safety glasses at all times when cutting egg. It is essential to work in a well ventilated area as dust is extremely fine and can be inhaled and could cause respiratory problems.)

FolkArt colour paint (matte spray finish paint is suitable for this work.) Wicker white. (It is essential to work in a well-ventilated, dust-free area when painting.)

Hairdryer

Narrow-neck vase (To position skewer for drying egg.)

Clear matte ceramic sealer (Duncan brand spray sealer is suitable for this work)

4B lead pencil (a soft 'B' pencil is required)

5 mm (³⁄₁₆") wide rubber band (this is a wide flat band)

Tape measure

Permanent marker (Artline superfine No. 725 pen is required. Any dark colour is suitable.)

Dome inset for top of egg (2.5 cm, 1 inch, oval shape)

Baby wipes (wet variety)

Diamond cutting wheel (size 7 mm ¼")

Dremel motor tool (see illustration)

Brass hinge (1 cm, ³⁄₈")

Stanley knife

Toothpicks (These are used for mixing and applying Araldite.)

Araldite (Only 5 minute epoxy resin glue is suitable to use.)

Glue (Aleene's Tacky glue is suitable to use)

2 m (2 yards) x 1 mm (¹⁄₂₀") fine gold braid

40 cm (16") square of rich red velvet

Scissors (fabric scissors)

Paint brush (1 cm FolkArt Angular Shader (This paint brush has a sloping head.)

2 m (2 yards) x 2 mm (¹⁄₁₀") gold braid with metallic single loop

26 mm (1") x 70 mm (2¾") gold egg stand

2 hinge covers (small decorative shape)

Triple leaf finding (1 x gold)

8 pearls (2 mm, $\frac{1}{10}$", no hole)

4 small gold flowers (5 mm, $\frac{3}{16}$")

TO DECORATE EGG SHELL

1. Constantly turn egg shell while spraying with paint. (Care is necessary to apply a thin coat of spray to prevent streaks forming.)

2. Using hairdryer, thoroughly dry paint. It is necessary to constantly turn skewer to dry evenly. Position skewer in a narrow-neck vase to cool egg after drying.

3. Repeat points 1 & 2 as many times as required. (Approximately 10 coats of paint are required, depending on surface condition of egg shell.) It is essential to thoroughly dry and cool egg between each coat of paint.

4. Spray twice with sealer. It is necessary to constantly turn skewer while applying spray. It is essential to thoroughly dry and cool egg between each application of sealer. Position skewer in a narrow-neck vase to cool egg after drying.

5. When cool, remove skewer.

6. It is essential to have pencil, large rubber band, tape measure and marker pen ready for the next step.

7. Hold egg shell up (longways) at eye level. Gauge where the centre of the top is and place a small mark with pencil. Turn egg around and mark centre of other end.

8. Place rubber band around shell, next to the 2 marks. Keep band flat. Position rubber band adjacent to marks. Using tape measure, ensure that band is positioned to divide egg shell into 2 even halves.

9. Using pencil, trace a fine line at edge of rubber band, around egg shell, over existing pencil marks. This will mark the centre line longways around the egg.

10. Using tape measure, mark a pencil line 1 cm ($\frac{3}{8}$") either side of centre line, around egg.

11. You now have to decide which will be the top and bottom of your jewellery box. Using marker pen, mark dots (approx. 1 mm, $\frac{1}{20}$" apart) on pencil line closest to bottom of jewellery box.

12. Mark lid of jewellery box by drawing another pencil line 2 cm ($\frac{4}{5}$") higher than centre line. Using this line as a guide, draw shape required for lid as illustrated.

13. Position dome in centre of lid. Using pencil, trace around dome. Remove dome and mark another line 1 mm ($\frac{1}{20}$") inside first line. This line will be the cutting line.

14. Mark lid shape outline and inside dome line with marker pen.

15. Using baby wipes, remove all pencil lines. Marker pen lines will remain.

16. Using marker pen, draw a 1 cm (³⁄₈") line vertically at centre back of lid for the position of the hinge.

17. Attach diamond cutting wheel to Dremel motor tool. Cut across vertical hinge line, approximately 5 cm (2"). (**Warning** — Wear face mask and safety glasses to perform this operation.)

18. Using cutting wheel, burr (roughen) back of hinge (to allow Araldite to adhere to it).

19. To prepare area for application of hinge, use Stanley knife and scrape paint from area where hinge is to be applied. It is important to remove all paint from this area, so Araldite is applied to bare egg shell. Also scrape rough edges of cut made by cutting wheel.

20. Using a toothpick, mix Araldite. Place Araldite onto back of hinge. Place hinge into position. Allow to dry for 24 hours.

21. Using cutting wheel, cut around line for dome. Cut around lid line. (**Warning** — Wear face mask and safety glasses to perform this operation.)

22. Gently open lid. Using Stanley knife scape rough edges of cutting lines.

23. Scrape around edges of cutting lines on inside of egg shell to remove membrane. Remove any pieces of membrane that are sticking up around inside shell. Do not remove all the membrane as this gives strength to the egg.

24. Place a small line of glue (Aleene's tacky glue) around inside top of lid. Secure fine gold braid to glue. Care is necessary to secure this in place.

25. Glue fine gold braid around inside opening for dome.

26. Glue fine gold braid to inside edge of base of jewellery box.

27. To cut velvet for inside bottom, place box on bias of fabric. Draw a pencil line 2.5 cm (1") wider than box. Draw a pencil line 1.5 cm (³⁄₅") wider than the lid. Cut velvet inside pencil lines.

28. Place some glue just under gold braid. Stick velvet into place. Take care to make sure folds of velvet are evenly positioned around inside of box.

29. Thin a little glue with water. Using brush, paint glue onto inside lid of box. Place velvet onto glue. Do not place velvet over braid. Cut velvet to shape of lid. Cut opening for dome.

30. Place a line of glue next to fine gold braid (on top of velvet). Position metallic loop braid onto glue. This will finish the inside of jewellery box.

31. Commence at hinge and run a

line of glue around the top out-side edge of box. Secure fine gold braid to glue.

32. Run a line of glue around bot-tom line on box. Secure fine gold braid to glue.

33. For the outside, cut a bias strip of velvet, wide and long enough to go around egg. (Length of strip will vary according to size of egg.)

34. Starting from the hinge, glue velvet onto egg shell the same way as for the inside top. Fabric cut on the bias can be posi-tioned easily around box.

35. Using brush, apply a small amount of glue to join. Secure and trim.

36. Apply gold braid (with metallic single loop) over velvet just under fine gold braid around top edge and base line of box.

37. Using toothpick, mix Araldite and place dome in position. Allow to dry.

38. Secure both braids around dome.

39. Using Araldite, position box onto stand; hinge covers onto hinge; leaf finding to top front; small pearls into flowers and flowers onto top of box. Glue one pearl into centre of dome and one into leaf finding and remaining 2 into holes on hinge covers.

Duck Egg with Angel Figurine

REQUIREMENTS

Duck egg, blown and prepared

Bisq Stain Opaque Acrylic Paint — Chiffon pink (Duncan brand is suitable for this work.)

Paint brush (1 cm, ⅜", FolkArt Angular Shader (This paint brush has a sloping head.)

Hairdryer

Narrow-neck vase (To position skewer for drying egg.)

Face mask (**Warning** — It is essen-tial to wear a mask at all times when painting and cutting egg.)

Safety glasses (**Warning** — It is essential to wear safety glasses at all times when cutting egg. It is essential to work in a well-venti-lated area as dust is extremely fine and can be inhaled and could cause respiratory problems.)

Clear matte ceramic sealer (Dun-can brand spray sealer is suitable for this work.)

4B lead pencil (A soft 'B' pencil is required.)

5 mm (³⁄₁₆") wide rubber band (This is a wide flat band.)

Tape measure

Permanent marker (Artline superfine No. 725 pen is required. Any dark colour is suitable.)

Dome inset for back of egg (2.5 cm, 1", oval shape)

Baby wipes (wet variety)

Diamond cutting wheel
(size 7 mm, ¼")

Dremel motor tool

Stanley knife

Glue (Aleene's Tacky glue is suitable to use.)

2 x 1 cm (¹⁄₂₀") diameter circles of white paper

0.5 m (20") x 1 mm, (¹⁄₂₀") fine gold braid

1 m (1 yard) x 2 mm (¹⁄₁₀") string pearls

0.5 m (20") x 2 mm (¹⁄₁₀") gold braid with metallic single loop

Toothpicks (These are used for mixing and applying Araldite.)

Araldite (Only 5 minute epoxy resin glue is suitable to use.)

Cut 2 cm (⅘") diameter circle soft cardboard (Size of circle will vary to fit inside of egg. This is used as a base for figurine.)

4 cm (1 ⅗") diameter circle of rich red velvet

Scissors (fabric scissors)

Angel figurine

Glue (Mod Podge glue is suitable for this work.)

Glitter (Disco dust)

1 gold egg stand (27 mm, 1", with 4 legs)

1 gold bead, (8mm, ⁵⁄₁₆")

1 x 5 cm (2") hat pin with round pearl end

1 small gold flower (1 cm, ⅜")

Styrene foam (1 small piece 15 cm, 6", thick)

TO DECORATE EGG SHELL

1. Constantly turn egg shell while applying paint. (Care is necessary to start at the top and go to bottom of egg in one smooth stroke. Do not use too much paint on brush as this will leave streaks.)

2. Using hairdryer, thoroughly dry paint. It is necessary to constantly turn skewer to dry evenly. Position skewer in a narrow-neck vase to cool egg after drying.

3. Repeat points 1 & 2 as many times as required. (Approximately 10 coats of paint are required, depending on surface condition of egg shell.) It is essential to thoroughly dry and cool egg between each coat of paint.

4. Spray twice with sealer. It is necessary to constantly turn skewer while applying spray. It is essential to thoroughly dry and cool egg between each application of sealer. Position skewer in a narrow-neck vase to cool egg after drying.

5. When cool, remove skewer.

6. It is essential to have pencil, large rubber band, tape measure and marker pen ready for the next step.

7. Hold egg shell up (longways) at eye level. Gauge where the centre of the top is and place a small mark with pencil. Turn egg around and mark centre of other end.

8. Place rubber band around shell, next to the 2 marks. Keep band flat. Position rubber band adjacent to marks. Using tape measure, ensure that band is positioned to divide egg shell into 2 even halves.

9. Using pencil, trace a fine line at edge of rubber band, around egg, over existing pencil marks. This will mark the centre line longways around the egg.

10. Select back of egg and place dome in centre. Using pencil, trace around dome. Remove dome and mark another line 1 mm (1/20") inside first line. This line will be the cutting line. Dot around this line with marker pen.

11. To shape front of egg, use a tape measure and draw a pencil line approximately 1 cm (3/8") from centre line. Curve this line up a little at the base, as it is necessary for this part of the egg shell to be secured to the stand. Dot around this line with marker pen.

12. Using baby wipes, remove all pencil lines. Marker pen lines will remain.

13. Attach diamond cutting wheel to Dremel motor tool. Cut around marker pen lines. (**Warning** — Wear face mask and safety glasses to perform this operation.)

14. Using Stanley knife scape rough edges of cutting lines.

15. Scrape around edges of cutting lines on inside of egg shell to remove membrane. Remove any pieces of membrane that are sticking up around inside shell. Do not remove all the membrane as this gives strength to the egg.

16. Glue (Aleene's tacky glue) circles of paper over inside of egg to cover holes.

17. Apply 2 coats of paint to inside of egg shell. Allow to dry and cool.

18. Starting from the bottom, glue fine gold braid to outside cut edge of egg shell.

19. Glue string of pearls next to fine gold braid.

20. Glue gold braid with metallic loop, next to pearls.

21. Using toothpick, mix Araldite and place dome in position. Allow to dry.

22. Using glue, position fine gold braid, string of pearls and metallic loop gold braid around dome.

23. Thin a little glue with water. Using brush, paint glue onto cardboard. Cover cardboard with velvet. Make sure velvet is secured to underside of cardboard for a neat finish.

24. Using Araldite, glue figurine onto centre of velvet. Allow to dry.

25. Paint inside of egg with Mod Podge glue. Do not allow any glue to go on the inside of the dome.

26. Sprinkle glitter thoroughly over glue. It is essential to work quickly as the glue dries almost immediately.

27. Position figurine into base of egg shell and secure with Araldite. Care is necessary to have figurine upright and centred.

28. Using Araldite, position egg onto stand. Allow to dry.

29. Using Araldite secure gold bead next to pearl end of hat pin and gold flower next to gold bead. Place point of pin into styrene foam and allow to dry.

30. Remove pin from styrene. Cut pin off just below gold flower. Araldite onto top of egg.

Goose Egg with Old English Decal

REQUIREMENTS TO DECORATE EGG

Goose egg (Follow instructions at the beginning of this chapter for the preparation of egg.)

Bisq Stain Opaque Acrylic Paint — pale blue (Duncan brand is suitable for this work.)

Paint brush (1 cm, ⅜" Folkart Angular Shader (This paint brush has a sloping head.)

Hairdryer

Narrow-neck vase (to position skewer for drying egg)

Face mask (**Warning** — It is essential to wear a mask at all times when painting and cutting egg.)

Safety glasses (**Warning** — It is essential to wear safety glasses at all times when cutting egg. It is essential to work in a well-ventilated area as dust is extremely fine and can be inhaled and could cause respiratory problems.)

Clear matte ceramic sealer (Duncan brand spray sealer is suitable for this work.)

4B lead pencil (a soft 'B' pencil is required.)

5 mm (³⁄₁₆") wide rubber band (This is a wide flat band.)

Tape measure

Permanent marker (Artline superfine No. 725 pen is required. Any dark colour is suitable.)

Brass hinge (1 cm, ⅜")

Baby wipes (wet variety)

Short fine pointed scissors

Old English decal

Small bowl and hot water (for removing decal from backing)

Tissues

Glue (Mod Podge glue is suitable for this work.)

Sandpaper (wet and dry, size 400 — 7 cm, 3" square)

Clean water

Diamond cutting wheel, (size 7 mm, ¼")

Dremel motor tool

Stanley knife

Toothpicks (These are used for mixing and applying Araldite.)

Araldite (Only 5 minute epoxy

resin glue is suitable to use.)

Glue (Aleene's Tacky glue is suitable to use.)

4 x 4 mm (³⁄₁₆") half circles white paper

Scissors (fabric scissors)

15 cm (6") square nylon wadding

2 m (2 yards) x 1 mm (¹⁄₂₀") fine gold braid

25 cm (10") square of floral taffeta

1 m (1 yard) x 5 mm (³⁄₁₆") white lace braid

1 m (1 yard) x 2 mm (¹⁄₁₀") string pearls

2 m (2 yards) x 2 mm (¹⁄₁₀") gold braid with metallic single loop

40 mm (1 ³⁄₅") x 50 mm (2") decorative gold egg stand

2 x 5 mm (³⁄₁₆") up-eyes

2 x 3 mm (¹⁄₈") jump rings

1 x 4.5 cm (2") fine gold chain

TO DECORATE EGG SHELL

1. Constantly turn egg shell while applying paint. (Care is necessary to start at the top and go to bottom of egg in one smooth stroke. Do not use too much paint on brush as this will leave streaks.)

2. Using hairdryer thoroughly dry paint. It is necessary to constantly turn skewer to dry evenly. Position skewer in a narrow-neck vase to cool egg after drying.

3. Repeat points 1 & 2 as many times as required. (Approximately 10 coats of paint are

required, depending on surface condition of egg shell.) It is essential to thoroughly dry and cool egg between each coat of paint.

4. Spray twice with sealer. It is necessary to constantly turn skewer while applying spray. It is essential to thoroughly dry and cool egg between each application of sealer. Position skewer in a narrow-neck vase to cool egg after drying.

5. When cool, remove skewer.

6. It is essential to have pencil, large rubber band, tape measure and marker pen ready for the next step.

7. Hold egg shell up (longways) at eye level. Gauge where the centre of the top is and place a small mark with pencil. Turn egg around and mark centre of other end.

8. Place rubber band around shell, next to the 2 marks. Keep band flat. Position rubber band adjacent to marks. Using tape measure, ensure that band is positioned to divide egg shell into 2 even halves.

9. Using pencil, trace a fine line at edge of rubber band, around egg, over existing pencil marks. This will mark the centre line longways around the egg.

10. Hold egg shell up again (longways) at eye level. Place a mark as if you were going to divide it into quarters. Take tape measure and mark from these 2

points along line just marked. Halve measurement and this should indicate centre front and back along first line. Using pencil, place a small mark at these points.

11. Move centre back marker to approximately 2 mm (1/10") towards the larger end of egg. This position is for the hinge and will make the egg shell open easier. Using marker pen, draw a 1 cm (3/8") line vertically at this point for the position of the hinge.

12. If you wish to have a curved line at the front of the egg, measure 1 cm (3/8") either side of centre front and mark with a pencil. Position a mark 5 mm (3/16") above the centre front mark. Pencil a curved line between these marks.

13. Using marker pen, mark dots (1 mm, 1/20" apart) on pencil line to be cut. Using baby wipes, remove all pencil lines. Marker pen line will remain.

14. Using sharp fine pointed scissors, cut as close as possible to picture on decal.

15. Place decal into a small bowl of hot water. When decal starts to lift from backing paper, it is ready to position on egg shell.

16. Remove decal from water. Slip decal off backing paper and onto top centre of egg shell. Take care as it is not easy to position a flat piece of paper onto the surface of a curved egg. Air bubbles will appear under the decal. These can be removed by using a tissue and wiping from the centre of the decal to the outside, positioning decal over the curve of the egg. (Care and perseverance are necessary for this application.)

17. It is now necessary to 'sink' the decal. To do this it is necessary to again place skewer through holes in egg. Thoroughly paint the whole of the egg shell with Mod Podge. Dry thoroughly with hairdryer. Repeat this process 5 times again, using 6 coats in total. Ensure egg shell is completely cool between each coat. Position skewer in a narrow-neck vase and allow egg to dry overnight.

18. Next day remove skewer. Using cool water and wet and dry sandpaper, sand surface of egg until smooth. Place skewer through holes in egg again and thoroughly dry with hairdryer. Allow to cool.

19. Thoroughly paint the whole of the egg shell with 6 more coats of Mod Podge, thoroughly drying with hairdryer between each coat. Position skewer in a narrow-neck vase and allow egg to dry overnight.

20. Next day remove skewer. Using cool water and wet and dry sandpaper, sand surface of egg until smooth. Place skewer through holes in egg again and thoroughly dry with hairdryer.

Allow to cool. Apply a further 6 coats of Mod Podge, thoroughly dry with hairdryer between each coat. Position skewer in a narrow-neck vase and allow egg to dry overnight. In total there are 18 coats of Mod Podge.

21. Next day remove skewer from egg. Using cool water and wet and dry sandpaper, sand surface of egg until smooth. Place skewer through holes in egg again and thoroughly dry with hairdryer. Allow egg to cool.

22. Spray twice with sealer. It is necessary to constantly turn skewer while applying spray. It is essential to thoroughly dry and cool egg between each application of sealer. Position skewer in a narrow-neck vase to cool egg after drying.

23. When cool, remove skewer.

24. Attach diamond cutting wheel to Dremel motor tool. Cut across vertical hinge line, approximately 5 cm (2"). (*Warning* — Wear face mask and safety glasses to perform this operation.)

25. Using cutting wheel, burr (roughen) back of hinge (to allow glue to adhere to it.)

26. To prepare area for application of hinge, use Stanley knife and scrape paint and glue from area where hinge is to be applied. It is important to remove all paint and glue from this area, so Araldite is applied to bare egg

shell. Also scrape rough edges of cut made by cutting wheel.

27. Using a toothpick, mix Araldite. Place Araldite onto back of hinge. Place hinge into position. Allow to dry for 24 hours.

28. Using diamond cutting wheel, cut around marker pen line. (*Warning*— Wear face mask and safety glasses to perform this operation.)

29. Using Stanley knife scrape rough edges of cutting lines.

30. Scrape around edges of cutting lines on inside of egg shell to remove membrane. Remove any pieces of membrane that are sticking up around inside shell. Do not remove all the membrane as this gives strength to the egg.

31. Glue (Aleene's Tacky glue) 2 half circles of paper over holes inside lid and 2 over holes inside bottom of egg. (These are the holes drilled in the preparation of the egg.)

32. Cut 2 oval pieces of wadding (3 cm, 1 3⁄16" x 5 cm, 2"). Using Aleene's Tacky glue position wadding into top and bottom of inside of jewellery box.

33. Starting at the front of the inside lip of the bottom of the jewellery box, glue on fine gold braid. Repeat with top of lid.

34. Close jewellery box and place on bias of taffeta. Using pencil, draw a line around egg shell

about 2.5 cm (1") larger than shell; 1 piece of taffeta for the top and 1 for the bottom. Cut taffeta just inside pencil line, so mark will not show on finished work.

35. Glue (Aleene's Tacky glue) taffeta, so that it is flush up against, but just underneath fine gold braid on the bottom of jewellery box. Taffeta will be larger than box and will need to be eased into small folds to fit shell. It is essential to glue each fold to egg shell, just under fine gold braid.

36. To position white lace braid, place a line of glue underneath gold braid making sure it is on top of taffeta. Position white lace braid.

37. Commencing at the hinge, glue (Aleene's Tacky glue) fine gold braid around outside top of jewellery box. Repeat for bottom.

38. Glue string of pearls so that it is flush up against, but just under gold braid.

39. Glue metallic loop gold braid flush up against, but just next to pearls.

40. Using Araldite, cover top and bottom of hinge with 3 rows of pearls on each.

41. Using Araldite, position jewellery box onto stand. Allow to dry for 24 hours.

42. Using Araldite, glue up-eyes inside on white lace braid in a

'9 o'clock' position on the bottom of the jewellery case and '10 o'clock' position on the top. Attach jump rings to ends of chain. Attach rings to up-eyes. This positioning will allow the chain to fall into the bottom of the jewellery case when it is closed.

Goose Egg with Pink Base, Cut-out Lid with Pearls and Gold Rose

REQUIREMENTS TO DECORATE EGG

Goose egg (Follow instructions at the beginning of this chapter for the preparation of egg.)

Bisq Stain Opaque Acrylic Paint — Chiffon pink (Duncan brand is suitable for this work.)

Paint brush (1 cm (⅜") FolkArt Angular Shader (This paint brush has a sloping head.)

Hairdryer

Narrow-neck vase (To position skewer for drying egg.)

Face mask (**Warning** — It is essential to wear a mask at all times when painting and cutting egg.)

Safety glasses (**Warning** — It is essential to wear safety glasses at all times when cutting egg. It is essential to work in a well-ventilated area as dust is extremely fine and can be inhaled and could cause respiratory problems.

Clear matte ceramic sealer (Duncan brand spray sealer is suitable for this work.)

4B lead pencil (A soft 'B' pencil is required.)

5 mm (³⁄₁₆") wide rubber band (This is a wide flat band.)

Tape measure

Permanent marker (Artline superfine No. 725 pen is required. Any dark colour is suitable.)

Brass hinge (1 cm, ³⁄₈")

Baby wipes (wet variety)

Diamond cutting wheel (size 7 mm, ¼")

Dremel motor tool

Stanley knife

Toothpicks (These are used for mixing and applying Araldite.)

Araldite (Only 5 minute epoxy resin glue is suitable to use.)

Glue (Aleene's Tacky glue is suitable to use.)

4 x 5 mm (³⁄₁₆") half circles white paper

Scissors (fabric scissors)

20 cm (8") square nylon wadding

6 m (6 yards) x 1 mm (¹⁄₂₀") fine gold braid

15 cm (6") square of white embossed taffeta

0.5 m (18") x 5 mm (³⁄₁₆") white lace braid

Glue (Mod Podge glue is suitable for this work.)

Glitter (Disco dust)

4 m (4 yards) x 2 mm (¹⁄₁₀") string pearls

1 m (1 yard) x 2 mm (¹⁄₁₀") gold braid with metallic single loop

40 mm (1 ³⁄₅") x 55 mm (2 ¹⁄₅") decorative gold egg stand

2 x 5 mm (³⁄₁₆") up-eyes

2 x 3 mm (⅛") jump rings

1 x 4.5 cm (1 ¹⁄₅") fine gold chain

1 gold finding (with 6 leaves)

1 gold finding (rose with 2 leaves)

1 small gold flower (1 cm, ³⁄₈")

TO DECORATE EGG SHELL

1. Constantly turn egg shell while applying paint. (Care is necessary to start at the top and go to bottom of egg in one smooth stroke. Do not use too much paint on brush as this will leave streaks.)

2. Using hairdryer thoroughly dry paint. It is necessary to constantly turn skewer to dry evenly. Position skewer in a narrow-neck vase to cool egg after drying.

3. Repeat points 1 & 2 as many times as required. (Approximately 10 coats of paint are required, depending on surface condition of egg shell.) It is essential to thoroughly dry and cool egg between each coat of paint.

4. Spray twice with sealer. It is necessary to constantly turn skewer while applying spray. It is essential to thoroughly dry and cool egg between each application of sealer. Position skewer in a narrow-neck vase to cool egg after drying.

5. When cool, remove skewer.

6. It is essential to have pencil, large rubber band, tape measure and marker pen ready for the next step.

7. Hold egg shell up (longways) at eye level. Gauge where the centre of the top is and place a small mark with pencil. Turn egg around and mark centre of other end.

8. Place rubber band around shell, next to the 2 marks. Keep band flat. Position rubber band adjacent to marks. Using tape measure, ensure that band is positioned to divide egg shell into 2 even halves.

9. Using pencil, trace a fine line at edge of rubber band, around egg, over existing pencil marks. This will mark the centre line longways around the egg.

10. Hold egg shell up again (longways) at eye level. Place a mark as if you were going to divide it into quarters. Take tape measure and mark from these 2 points along line just marked. Halve measurement and this should indicate centre front and back along first line. Using pencil, place a small mark at these points.

11. Move centre back marker to approximately 2 mm ($\frac{1}{10}$") towards the larger end of egg. This position is for the hinge and will make the egg shell open easier. Using marker pen, draw a 1 cm ($\frac{3}{8}$") line vertically

at this point for the position of the hinge.

12. Using pencil mark centre of top of egg in half, longways and crossways. Mark halfway between these lines. Position sections evenly around top of egg shell. Draw in shapes required leaving approximately 5 mm ($\frac{3}{16}$") between each section.

13. Using pencil, position a 1 cm ($\frac{3}{8}$") circle on top of egg shell. This will be the position for the gold rose.

14. Using marker pen, mark dots (1 mm, $\frac{1}{20}$", apart) on pencil lines to be cut. Using baby wipes, remove all pencil lines. Marker pen line will remain.

15. Attach diamond cutting wheel to Dremel motor tool. Cut across vertical hinge line, approximately 5 cm (2"). (**Warning** — Wear face mask and safety glasses to perform this operation.)

16. Using cutting wheel, burr (roughen) back of hinge (to allow glue to adhere to it.)

17. To prepare area for application of hinge, use Stanley knife and scrape paint from area where hinge is to be applied. It is important to remove all paint from this area, so Araldite is applied to bare egg shell. Also scrape rough edges of cut made by cutting wheel.

18. Using a toothpick, mix Araldite. Place Araldite onto

back of hinge. Place hinge into position. Allow to dry for 24 hours.

19. Using diamond cutting wheel, cut around marker pen line. (**Warning** — Wear face mask and safety glasses to perform this operation.)

20. Using Stanley knife scrape rough edges of cutting lines.

21. Scrape around edges of cutting lines on inside of egg shell to remove membrane. Remove any pieces of membrane that are sticking up around inside shell. Do not remove all the membrane as this gives strength to the egg.

22. Glue (Aleene's Tacky glue) 2 half circles of paper over holes inside lid and 2 over holes inside bottom of egg. (These are the holes drilled in the preparation of the egg.)

23. Mix Araldite and apply to inside top of egg shell. Leave to dry. This will strengthen top.

24. Apply 2 coats of paint to inside top of egg shell. Dry with hairdryer and allow to cool.

25. Cut oval of wadding (3 cm, $1\frac{1}{10}$" x 5 cm, 2"). Using Aleene's Tacky glue position wadding into bottom of jewellery box.

26. Starting at the front of the inside lip of the bottom of the jewellery box, glue on fine gold braid. Repeat with top of lid.

27. Close jewellery box and place on bias of taffeta. Using pencil, draw a line around egg shell about 2.5 cm (1") larger than bottom of shell. Cut taffeta just inside pencil line, so mark will not show on finished work.

28. Glue (Aleene's Tacky glue) taffeta, so that it is flush up against, but just underneath fine gold braid on the bottom of jewellery box. Taffeta will be larger than box and will need to be eased into small folds to fit shell. It is essential to glue each fold to egg shell, just under fine gold braid.

29. To position white lace braid, place a line of glue underneath gold braid making sure it is on top of taffeta. Position white lace braid.

30. Paint inside of top of egg shell with Mod Podge glue.

31. Sprinkle glitter thoroughly over glue. It is essential to work quickly as the glue dries almost immediately.

32. Commencing at the hinge, glue (Aleene's Tacky glue) fine gold braid around outside top of jewellery box. Repeat for bottom.

33. Glue string of pearls so that it is flush up against, but just under gold braid.

34. Glue gold braid with metallic single loop, flush up against, but just next to pearls, on bottom of jewellery box.

35. Glue fine gold braid around cut out section on lid.

36. Glue string of pearls flush up against, but just under fine gold braid.

37. Using Araldite, cover top and bottom of hinge with 3 rows of pearls.

38. Paint Mod Podge glue between 2 rows of pearls at the lid opening of the top of the jewellery box. Sprinkle glitter thoroughly over glue.

39. Using Araldite, position jewellery box onto stand. Allow to dry.

40. Using Araldite, glue up-eyes inside on white lace braid in a '9 o'clock' position on the bottom of the jewellery case and '10 o'clock' position on the top. Attach jump rings to ends of chain. Attach rings to up-eyes. This positioning will allow the chain to fall into the bottom of the jewellery case when it is closed.

41. Using Araldite, position gold leaf findings and rose onto centre top of lid.

42. Using Araldite, position small gold flower onto centre top inside of lid.

Duck Egg with Rhinestones on Swan Stand

REQUIREMENTS TO DECORATE EGG

Duck egg (Follow instructions at the beginning of this chapter for the preparation of egg.)

Face mask (**Warning** — It is essential to wear a mask at all times when painting and cutting egg.)

Safety glasses (**Warning** — It is essential to wear safety glasses at all times when cutting egg. It is essential to work in a well-ventilated area as dust is extremely fine and can be inhaled and could cause respiratory problems.)

FolkArt colour paint (FolkArt colour matte spray finish paint is suitable for this work.)

Colour required — Wicker white. (It is essential to work in a well-ventilated, dust-free area when painting.)

Hairdryer

Clear matte ceramic sealer (Duncan brand spray sealer is suitable for this work.)

Narrow-neck vase (To position skewer for drying egg.)

4B lead pencil (A soft 'B' pencil is required.)

5 mm ($\frac{3}{16}$") wide rubber band (This is a wide flat band.)

Tape measure

Permanent marker (Artline superfine No. 725 pen is required. Any dark colour is suitable.)

Baby wipes (wet variety)

Diamond cutting wheel (size 7 mm, $\frac{1}{4}$")

Dremel motor tool

Brass hinge (1 cm, $\frac{3}{8}$")

Stanley knife

Toothpicks (These are used for

mixing and applying Araldite.)

Araldite (Only 5 minute epoxy resin glue is suitable to use.)

Glue (Aleene's Tacky glue is suitable to use.)

2 x 1 cm (⅜") diameter circles of white paper

Scissors (fabric scissors)

30 cm (12") square nylon wadding

2 m (2 yards) x 1 mm (1/20") gold braid

6 cm (2⅖") square of white embossed taffeta

0.5 m (18") x 5 mm (3/16") white lace braid

1 m (1 yard) x 2 mm (1/10") rhinestones chain setting

1 m (1 yard) x 2 mm (1/10") gold braid with metallic single loop

Swan decorative gold egg stand (60 mm, 2 ⅖", high)

1 gold flower (1 cm, ⅜")

2 small gold flowers (5 mm, 3/16")

TO DECORATE EGG SHELL

1. Constantly turn egg shell while applying paint.

2. Using hairdryer thoroughly dry paint. It is necessary to constantly turn skewer to dry evenly. Position skewer in a narrow-neck vase to cool egg after drying.

3. Repeat points 1 & 2 as many times as required. (Approximately 10 coats of paint are required, depending on surface condition of egg shell.) It is essential to thoroughly dry and cool egg between each coat of paint.

4. Spray twice with sealer. It is necessary to constantly turn skewer while applying spray. It is essential to thoroughly dry and cool egg between each application of sealer. Position skewer in a narrow-neck vase to cool egg after drying.

5. When cool, remove skewer.

6. It is essential to have pencil, large rubber band, tape measure and marker pen ready for the next step.

7. Hold egg shell up (longways) at eye level. Gauge where the centre of the top is and place a small mark with pencil. Turn egg around and mark centre of other end.

8. Place rubber band around shell, next to the 2 marks. Keep band flat. Position rubber band adjacent to marks. Using tape measure, ensure that band is positioned to divide egg shell into 2 even halves.

9. Using pencil, trace a fine line at edge of rubber band, around egg, over existing pencil marks. This will mark the centre line longways around the egg.

10. Hold egg shell up again (longways) at eye level. Place a mark as if you were going to divide it into quarters. Put rubber band around these marks and mark into quarters again. Take tape measure and mark from these 2 points along line just marked.

Halve measurement and this should indicate centre front and back along first line. Using pencil, place a small mark at these points. Curve line for lid opening to shape required.

11. Mark the centre back of egg. This position is for the hinge. Using marker pen, draw a 1 cm (⅜") line vertically at this point for the position of the hinge.

12. Using marker pen, mark dots (1 mm, ¹⁄₂₀", apart) on pencil line to be cut. Using baby wipes, remove all pencil lines. Marker pen line will remain.

13. Attach diamond cutting wheel to Dremel motor tool. Cut across vertical hinge line, approximately 5 cm (2"). (*Warning* — Wear face mask and safety glasses to perform this operation.)

14. Using cutting wheel, burr (roughen) back of hinge (to allow glue to adhere to it.)

15. To prepare area for application of hinge, use Stanley knife and scrape paint from area where hinge is to be applied. It is important to remove all paint from this area, so Araldite is applied to bare egg shell. Also scrape rough edges of cut made by cutting wheel.

16. Using a toothpick, mix Araldite. Place Araldite onto back of hinge. Place hinge into position. Allow to dry for 24 hours.

17. Using diamond cutting wheel, cut around marker pen line. (*Warning* — Wear face mask and safety glasses to perform this operation.)

18. Using Stanley knife scrape rough edges of cutting lines.

19. Scrape around edges of cutting lines on inside of egg shell to remove membrane. Remove any pieces of membrane that are sticking up around inside shell. Do not remove all the membrane as this gives strength to the egg.

20. Glue (Aleene's Tacky glue) 1 piece paper over hole inside lid and 1 over hole inside bottom of egg. (These are the holes drilled in the preparation of the egg.)

21. Cut 2 circles of wadding (2 cm, ⅘", diameter). Using Aleene's Tacky glue position wadding into bottom and top of inside of jewellery box.

22. Starting at the front of the inside lip of the bottom of the jewellery box, glue on fine gold braid. Repeat with top of lid.

23. Close jewellery box and place on bias of taffeta. Using pencil, draw a line around egg shell about 2.5 cm (1") larger than bottom of shell. Cut taffeta just inside pencil line, so mark will not show on finished work. Repeat for lid.

24. Glue (Aleene's Tacky glue) taffeta, so that it is flush up against, but just underneath fine gold braid on the bottom

of jewellery box. Taffeta will be larger than box and will need to be eased into small folds to fit shell. It is essential to glue each fold to egg shell, just under fine gold braid.

25. To position white lace braid, place a line of glue underneath gold braid making sure it is on top of taffeta. Position white lace braid for top and bottom of jewellery box.

26. Commencing at the hinge, glue (Aleene's Tacky glue) fine gold braid around outside top of jewellery box. Repeat for bottom.

27. Using Araldite, glue rhinestones so that they are flush up against, but just under gold braid, on top and bottom of fine gold braid.

28. Glue metallic loop gold braid flush up against, but just next to rhinestones, on top and bottom of jewellery box.

29. Using Araldite, cover top and bottom of hinge with 4 rows of rhinestones. Two lots of 4 stones and then 2 above, with 1 at the top of hinge.

30. Using Araldite, position jewellery box onto stand. Allow to dry.

31. Using Araldite, position rhinestones around base of egg at top of stand. Allow to dry.

32. Using Araldite, position gold flower (1 cm, ⅜") on centre top of lid.

33. Using Araldite, glue 1 rhinestone into the centre of each of the 2 small gold flowers. Glue one into gold flower on top of lid and the other at the centre front opening.

Duck Egg with Gold Findings and Pearls

REQUIREMENTS TO DECORATE EGG

Duck egg (Follow instructions at the beginning of this chapter for the preparation of egg.)

Bisq Stain Opaque Acrylic Paint - Chiffon pink (Duncan brand is suitable for this work.)

Paint brush (1 cm, ⅜" FolkArt Angular Shader — this paint brush has a sloping head.)

Hairdryer

Narrow-neck vase (To position skewer for drying egg.)

Face mask (**Warning** — It is essential to wear a mask at all times when painting and cutting egg.)

Safety glasses (**Warning** — It is essential to wear safety glasses at all times when cutting egg. It is essential to work in a well-ventilated area as dust is extremely fine and can be inhaled and could cause respiratory problems.)

Clear matte ceramic sealer (Duncan brand spray sealer is suitable for this work.)

4B lead pencil (A soft 'B' pencil is required.)

5 mm (³⁄₁₆") wide rubber band (This

is a wide flat band.)

Tape measure

Permanent marker (Artline superfine No. 725 pen is required. Any dark colour is suitable.)

Baby wipes (wet variety)

Diamond cutting wheel (size 7 mm, ¼")

Dremel motor tool

Brass hinge (1 cm, ⅜")

Stanley knife

Toothpicks (These are used for mixing and applying Araldite.)

Araldite (Only 5 minute epoxy resin glue is suitable to use.)

Glue (Aleene's Tacky glue is suitable to use.)

4 x 5 mm (³⁄₁₆") half circles white paper

Scissors (fabric scissors)

15 cm (6") square nylon wadding

2 m (2 yards) x 1 mm (¹⁄₂₀") fine gold braid

25 cm (10") square of embossed taffeta

1 m (1 yard) x 5 mm (³⁄₁₆") white lace braid

1 m (1 yard) x 2 mm (¹⁄₁₀") string pearls

0.5 m (18") x 2 mm (¹⁄₁₀") gold braid with metallic single loop

25 mm (10") x 55 mm (2 ⅕") decorative gold egg stand

1 small gold butterfly

1 small gold leaf finding (3 leaves)

8 small gold flowers (8 mm, ⅛")

8 small pearls (2 mm, ¹⁄₁₀", no hole)

TO DECORATE EGG SHELL

1. Constantly turn egg shell while applying paint. (Care is necessary to start at the top and go to bottom of egg in one smooth stroke. Do not use too much paint on brush as this will leave streaks.)

2. Using hairdryer thoroughly dry paint. It is necessary to constantly turn skewer to dry evenly. Position skewer in a narrow-neck vase to cool egg after drying.

3. Repeat points 1 & 2 as many times as required. (Approximately 10 coats of paint are required, depending on surface condition of egg shell.) It is essential to thoroughly dry and cool egg between each coat of paint.

4. Spray twice with sealer. It is necessary to constantly turn skewer while applying spray. It is essential to thoroughly dry and cool egg between each application of sealer. Position skewer in a narrow-neck vase to cool egg after drying.

5. When cool, remove skewer.

6. It is essential to have pencil, large rubber band, tape measure and marker pen ready for the next step.

7. Hold egg shell up (longways) at eye level. Gauge where the centre of the top is and place a small mark with pencil. Turn egg around and mark centre of other end.

8. Place rubber band around shell, next to the 2 marks. Keep band flat. Position rubber band adjacent to marks. Using tape measure, ensure that band is positioned to divide egg shell into 2 even halves.

9. Using pencil, trace a fine line at edge of rubber band, around egg, over existing pencil marks. This will mark the centre line longways around the egg.

10. Hold egg shell up again (longways) at eye level. Place a mark as if you were going to divide it into quarters. Take tape measure and mark from these 2 points along line just marked. Halve measurement and this should indicate centre front and back along first line. Using pencil, place a small mark at these points.

11. Move centre back marker to approximately 2 mm ($\frac{1}{10}$") towards the larger end of egg. This position is for the hinge and will make the egg shell open easier. Using marker pen, draw a 1 cm ($\frac{3}{8}$") line vertically at this point for the position of the hinge.

12. If you wish to have a curved line at the front of the egg, measure 1 cm ($\frac{3}{8}$") either side of centre front and mark with a pencil. Position a mark 5 mm ($\frac{3}{16}$") above the centre front mark. Pencil a curved line between these marks.

13. Using marker pen, mark dots (1

mm, $\frac{1}{20}$", apart) on pencil line to be cut. Using baby wipes, remove all pencil lines. Marker pen line will remain.

14. Attach diamond cutting wheel to Dremel motor tool. Cut across vertical hinge line, approximately 5 cm (2"). (**Warning** — Wear face mask and safety glasses to perform this operation.)

15. Using cutting wheel, burr (roughen) back of hinge (to allow glue to adhere to it.)

16. To prepare area for application of hinge, use Stanley knife and scrape paint from area where hinge is to be applied. It is important to remove all paint from this area, so Araldite is applied to bare egg shell. Also scrape rough edges of cut made by cutting wheel.

17. Using a toothpick, mix Araldite. Place Araldite onto back of hinge. Place hinge into position. Allow to dry for 24 hours.

18. Using diamond cutting wheel, cut around marker pen line. (**Warning** — Wear face mask and safety glasses to perform this operation.)

19. Using Stanley knife scrape rough edges of cutting lines.

20. Scrape around edges of cutting lines on inside of egg shell to remove membrane. Remove any pieces of membrane that are sticking up around inside shell. Do not remove all the

membrane as this gives strength to the egg.

21. Glue (Aleene's Tacky glue) 2 pieces of paper over holes inside lid and 2 over holes inside bottom of egg. (These are the holes drilled in the preparation of the egg.)

22. Cut 2 oval pieces of wadding (2 cm, ⅘", x 3 cm, 1 ¹⁄₁₀"). Using Aleene's Tacky glue position wadding into top and bottom of inside of jewellery box.

23. Starting at the front of the inside lip of the bottom of the jewellery box, glue on fine gold braid. Repeat with top of lid.

24. Close jewellery box and place on bias of taffeta. Using pencil, draw a line around egg shell about 2.5 cm (1") larger than shell; 1 piece of taffeta for the top and 1 for the bottom. Cut taffeta just inside pencil line, so mark will not show on finished work.

25. Glue (Aleene's Tacky glue) taffeta, so that it is flush up against, but just underneath fine gold braid on the bottom of jewellery box. Taffeta will be larger than box and will need to be eased into small folds to fit shell. It is essential to glue each fold to egg shell, just under fine gold braid.

26. To position white lace braid, place a line of glue underneath fine gold braid making sure it is on top of taffeta. Position white lace braid.

27. Commencing at the hinge, glue (Aleene's Tacky glue) fine gold braid around outside top of jewellery box. Repeat for bottom.

28. Glue string of pearls so that it is flush up against, but just under gold braid.

29. Glue gold braid with metallic single loop, flush up against, but just next to pearls.

30. Using Araldite, cover top and bottom of hinge with 4 rows of pearls. Start with 5 pearls in the row closest to the hinge, finishing with 2 at the top and bottom row.

31. Using Araldite, position jewellery box onto stand. Allow to dry for 24 hours.

32. Glue gold butterfly, gold flowers and gold findings in position required on lid of jewellery box.

33. Araldite pearls (no holes) into centres of flowers.

Duck Egg with Heart Shaped Dome

REQUIREMENTS TO DECORATE EGG

Duck egg (Follow instructions at the beginning of this chapter for the preparation of egg.)

Bisq Stain Opaque Acrylic Paint — chiffon pink (Duncan brand is suitable for this work.)

Paint brush (1 cm, ⅜", FolkArt

Angular Shader (This paint brush has a sloping head.)

Hairdryer

Narrow-neck vase (To position skewer for drying egg.)

Face mask (**Warning** — It is essential to wear a mask at all times when painting and cutting egg.)

Safety glasses (**Warning** — It is essential to wear safety glasses at all times when cutting egg. It is essential to work in a well-ventilated area as dust is extremely fine and can be inhaled and could cause respiratory problems.)

Clear matte ceramic sealer (Duncan brand spray sealer is suitable for this work.)

4B lead pencil (A soft 'B' pencil is required.)

5 mm (³⁄₁₆") wide rubber band (This is a wide flat band.)

Tape measure

1 small heart dome

Permanent marker (Artline superfine No. 725 pen is required. Any dark colour is suitable.)

Baby wipes (wet variety)

Diamond cutting wheel (size 7 mm, ¼")

Dremel motor tool

Brass hinge (1 cm, ³⁄₈")

Stanley knife

Toothpicks (These are used for mixing and applying Araldite.)

Araldite (Only 5 minute epoxy resin glue is suitable to use.)

Glue (Aleene's Tacky glue is suit-

able to use.)

4 x 5 mm (³⁄₁₆") half circles white paper

Scissors (fabric scissors)

10 cm (4") square nylon wadding

2 m (2 yards) x 2 mm (¹⁄₁₀") small white & gold braid

15 cm (6") square of pink taffeta

Glue (Mod Podge glue is suitable for this work.)

Glitter (Disco dust)

1 m (1 yard) x 5 mm (³⁄₁₆") pink lace braid

1 m (1 yard) x 2 mm (¹⁄₁₀") string pearls

1 m (1 yard) x 2 mm (¹⁄₁₀") gold braid with metallic single loop

7 x small pearls (2 mm, ¹⁄₁₀", no hole)

25 mm (1") x 55 mm (2 ¹⁄₅") decorative gold egg stand

TO DECORATE EGG SHELL

1. Constantly turn egg shell while applying paint. (Care is necessary to start at the top and go to bottom of egg in one smooth stroke. Do not use too much paint on brush as this will leave streaks.)

2. Using hairdryer thoroughly dry paint. It is necessary to constantly turn skewer to dry evenly. Position skewer in a narrow-neck vase to cool egg after drying.

3. Repeat points 1 & 2 as many times as required. (Approximately 10 coats of paint are

required, depending on surface condition of egg shell.) It is essential to thoroughly dry and cool egg between each coat of paint.

4. Spray twice with sealer. It is necessary to constantly turn skewer while applying spray. It is essential to thoroughly dry and cool egg between each application of sealer. Position skewer in a narrow-neck vase to cool egg after drying.

5. When cool, remove skewer.

6. It is essential to have pencil, large rubber band, tape measure and marker pen ready for the next step.

7. Hold egg shell up (longways) at eye level. Gauge where the centre of the top is and place a small mark with pencil. Turn egg around and mark centre of other end.

8. Place rubber band around shell, next to the 2 marks. Keep band flat. Position rubber band adjacent to marks. Using tape measure, ensure that band is positioned to divide egg shell into 2 even halves.

9. Using pencil, trace a fine line at edge of rubber band, around egg, over existing pencil marks. This will mark the centre line longways around the egg.

10. Hold egg shell up again (longways) at eye level. Place a mark as if you were going to divide it into quarters. Take tape measure and mark from these 2

points along line just marked. Halve measurement and this should indicate centre front and back along first line. Using pencil, place a small mark at these points.

11. Gently bend dome to allow it to sit better on curve of egg. Select top of egg and place dome in centre. Using pencil, trace around dome. Remove dome and mark another line approx. 1 mm ($\frac{1}{20}$") inside first line. This line will be the cutting line. Dot around this line with marker pen.

12. Move centre back marker to approximately 2 mm ($\frac{1}{10}$") towards the larger end of egg. This position is for the hinge and will make the egg shell open easier. Using marker pen, draw a 1 cm ($\frac{3}{8}$") line vertically at this point for the position of the hinge.

13. Using marker pen, mark dots (approx. 1 mm, $\frac{1}{20}$", apart) on pencil lines to be cut. Using baby wipes, remove all pencil lines. Marker pen line will remain.

14 Attach diamond cutting wheel to Dremel motor tool. Cut across vertical hinge line, approximately 5 cm (2"). (**Warning** — Wear face mask and safety glasses to perform this operation.)

15. Using cutting wheel, burr (roughen) back of hinge (to allow glue to adhere to it.)

16. To prepare area for application of hinge, use Stanley knife and scrape paint from area where hinge is to be applied. It is important to remove all paint from this area, so Araldite is applied to bare egg shell. Also scrape rough edges of cut made by cutting wheel.

17. Using a toothpick, mix Araldite. Place Araldite onto back of hinge. Place hinge into position. Allow to dry for 24 hours.

18. Using diamond cutting wheel, cut around marker pen line. (**Warning** — Wear face mask and safety glasses to perform this operation.)

19. Using Stanley knife scrape rough edges of cutting lines.

20. Scrape around edges of cutting lines on inside of egg shell to remove membrane. Remove any pieces of membrane that are sticking up around inside shell. Do not remove all the membrane as this gives strength to the egg.

21. Glue (Aleene's Tacky glue) 2 pieces of paper over holes inside lid and 2 over holes inside bottom of egg. (These are the holes drilled in the preparation of the egg.)

22. Cut an oval piece of wadding (2 cm, ⅘" x 3 cm, 1 ⅕"). Using Aleene's Tacky glue position wadding into bottom inside of jewellery box.

23. Starting at the front of the inside lip of the bottom of the jewellery box, glue on small white and gold braid. Repeat with top of lid.

24. Close jewellery box and place on bias of taffeta. Using pencil, draw a line around egg shell about 2.5 cm (1") larger than bottom of shell. Cut taffeta just inside pencil line, so mark will not show on finished work.

25. Glue (Aleene's Tacky glue) taffeta, so that it is flush up against, but just underneath white and gold braid on bottom of jewellery box. Taffeta will be larger than box and will need to be eased into small folds to fit shell. It is essential to glue each fold to egg shell just under white and gold braid.

26. Paint inside of lid with Mod Podge glue.

27. Sprinkle glitter thoroughly over glue. It is essential to work quickly as the glue dries almost immediately.

28. To position pink lace braid, place a line of glue underneath white and gold braid making sure it is on top of taffeta. Position pink lace braid.

29. Using glue position pink lace braid next to white and gold braid on the inside of the lid.

30. Commencing at the hinge, glue (Aleene's Tacky glue) small white and gold braid around outside top of jewellery box. Repeat for bottom.

31. Glue string of pearls so that it is flush up against, but just under white and gold braid.

32. Glue gold braid with metallic single loop flush up against, but just next to pearls.

33. Using Araldite, place dome in position. Allow to dry.

34. Using glue, position white and gold braid around dome.

35. Using glue, position string of pearls next to white and gold braid.

36. Using glue, position gold braid with metallic single loop next to pearls.

37. Using Araldite, position pearls (no hole) onto dome.

38. Using Araldite, cover top and bottom of hinge with 4 rows of pearls. Start with 5 pearls in the row closest to the hinge, finishing with 2 at the top and bottom row.

39. Using Araldite, position jewellery box onto stand. Allow to dry for 24 hours.

DÉCOUPAGE

DESIGNED AND WORKED BY VAL LADE

Découpage is the creative art of decorating hard surfaces with paper cut-outs. The French word 'découper' means 'to cut'. This is how the craft gets its name. The artform was practised widely in Venice in the seventeenth century, with a resurgence within the French Courts just before the French Revolution. In England, the craft flourished during the reign of Queen Victoria. Découpage faded from English life during the First World War and from French lifestyle during the French Revolution. It died out in Venice, the place of its birth, with the entry of Napoleon. But over the centuries découpage has been revived in many different forms and is popular again today.

Surfaces of eggs to be decorated must be thoroughly prepared. Pictures must be cut out accurately and glued down separately with even distribution of glue. Any excess glue must be removed from above and beneath the cut-outs. Success with the surface depends on the application of many finely-coated applications of varnish (up to 30 coats) which need to be sanded frequently to achieve a flat, smooth surface. The finished product is then waxed to produce a mellow finish.

Prints for découpage are best if they are on thin paper. Gift wrapping paper of a consistent quality and colour is suitable for work on eggs, however they need to be sealed to prevent colours 'bleeding'. Do not use paper that has been folded. If possible pictures from books specifically for découpage are best to use by those starting the craft for the first time. Avoid using glossy magazines, embossed papers, cards, thin porous and glossy papers and foil. Collate the pictures you select for your eggs into shapes and sizes to fit the egg. Consider themes and colours for each egg.

Eighteenth Century Découpage Eggs

There are three (3) special considerations when working découpage on eggs;

1. An egg has a curved shape, which means lots of cutting into

the image is necessary to make it fit the curve.

2. An egg has a surprising amount of surface area to cover.

3. It is quick and easy to lacquer eggs as they can be dipped into the lacquer.

BLOWING THE EGGS

Follow the instructions given on page 5 for blowing the eggs. Blown eggs are definitely suited to this work as the creations made will become treasured heirlooms.

DECORATING THE EGG

Requirements

acrylic paints (Liquitex Acrylic paints are suitable to use)

COLOURS FOR BAT FAIRY

Background colour: Burnt Umber and copper at base phased into Iridescent Gold at the top, applied with a sea-sponge.)

COLOURS FOR FAIRIES WITH DEW-DROP BALLS

Background colour: Acra Violet, Copper and Gold worked with damp sea-sponge from dark to light.

sea sponge

Liquitex Gloss Medium and Varnish

Suitable images — Ida Rentoul Outhwaite fairies are used here.

Images for the Bat Fairy are: fairy, moon, clouds, birds, dragonflies, flowers and toadstools

Images for the Fairies with Dew-

drop balls are: fairy, rabbit, flower and mouse

Small, sharp scissors, preferably with a curved blade

Blu-tack

Ice cream container lid (to use as palette)

Shaslik stick

00 paint brush

Lacquer

320 sandpaper, wrapped around block

Micromesh kit (optional)

PVA glue

Method

1. Cut out design and Blu-tack it on so that you can decide what paint you will use to obtain the mood you wish to create.

2. Acrylic paints are most suitable for découpage. They dry quickly and remain stable in changing climatic conditions. They can be thinned with polymer medium or water. These paints dry quickly because the chemical structure has a porosity that allows complete evaporation to occur. They have strong adhesion and each layer binds itself well to the one underneath. Research also suggests that they are resistant to oxidising and chemical breakdown. Care is necessary when squeezing from a tube as a certain amount of paint collects around the nozzle. This paint hardens, preventing the cap closing tightly. Air can

infiltrate the paint causing it to either harden or liquefy.

3. Acrylic paints are applied with a sea-sponge. This gives a textured feel and an added dimension. Acrylic paint dries very quickly so as soon as you have finished painting, wash sponge thoroughly in water to remove every bit of remaining paint. When all the water is removed, allow to thoroughly dry. If any paint is missed and dries hard, it will be necessary to soak the sponge in methylated spirits for 12 hours and then work the paint out with your fingers. If this does not work, leave sponge in nail varnish remover for 15 minutes. Finally wash well in warm soapy water and rinse with cold water until all soap residue is removed. Dry thoroughly. An ice cream carton lid makes a simple palette. It is flat and takes a number of colours and allows the sponge to move easily. Any unused paint can be stored by putting a small piece of wet sponge in an ice cream carton and replacing the lid with the paint still on the lid. It will keep moist for days when stored in this way.

4. When painting, the best way to hold the egg is at each end between your finger and thumb. This gives a firm hold and makes you feel in control of your work. The ends will have no paint where your thumb and finger were. To paint these areas, insert the blunt end of a shashlik stick in the larger hole, pushing it gently up to the top. Hold the stick and paint the missed areas. Poke the sharp end of the stick into a jar of sand or rice and allow the paint to dry for 24 hours. Some small holes can be drilled into an old block of wood to hold the stick. Do not use florist's foam as it is dissolved by lacquer.

5. Remember the image must be coaxed to curve by cutting. By holding the fairy against the egg and pressing the image gently into place you will form a good idea of where an extra cutting should be.

Use the rules below as your guide when cutting into the design.

- At all costs, avoid faces. Cut around the hair line or chin, but leave the face alone. It is too hard to repair if it is damaged.

- The major cutting will be needed around the widest areas.

- Where possible, cut along an existing line. In this case, cut along the lines between the cape and dress and into the hair of the fairy.

- It is better to over-cut rather than not have enough cuts.

6. Remove the stick from the egg and glue the main images with Liquitex Gloss Medium and Varnish. Gluing needs to be looked at logically. Dress fabric must for instance not overlap. Place a good quantity of Gloss

Medium and Varnish on the egg where the image is to go. Use a 00 brush and gently position the cut-out, making sure the right things overlap. When you are happy with the positioning, gently push the image into place with a damp piece of sponge until it is secured. If you have a doubt about an area, invert a brush and use the other end as a miniature roller.

7. Clean up and allow the glue to dry before you proceed to the next cut-out. It is important to work patiently on a curved surface of the egg, otherwise your fingers may stick to undried glue at the back of the egg and damage the image. Each piece of glue work must be touch-dry (approx. 5-10 minutes) before proceeding.

8. When everything is glued in place and dry, replace the egg on the stick. Stand the stick upright and seal with 2 coats of Gloss Medium and Varnish. Allow 1 hour drying time for each coat. Try and concentrate some of the sealant around the area at the bottom where the stick enters the egg. This will help bond the stick and egg.

LACQUERING

1. If the stick has not bonded to the egg, the first dipping into the tin of lacquer will have to be done with great care. Immerse the egg in the lacquer.

After immersing the egg right into the lacquer, hold the stick at a slight angle so the lacquer runs off the egg, not at the very end, but at a point towards it. Let all the lacquer run off. It is important to work quickly and the very second that the run of lacquer develops into a drip, twist the stick around, invert the egg and stand the stick upright in a container so that the lacquer can run down the egg to the stick in the opposite direction. If you delay during this procedure and wait until there are several drips, the lacquer will already have begun to dry slightly and it will not run easily in the opposite direction down to the stick. It will resist the change of direction and be sluggish, not reaching the stick but forming a drip. It is necessary for the lacquer to be fluid enough to prevent drips and runs. Do not use old lacquer which may have thickened. The first dip adheres the egg to the stick, so subsequent dips are quick and easy.

2. Dip the egg 5 times before sanding with No. 320 sandpaper wrapped around a block. Leave the egg on the stick while doing this. A good firm foam block is suitable. Good quality sandpaper is essential. Use light even applications. Sanding is very important to remove any imperfections. It provides the base to enable the next coat to bond.

German stearate sandpapers with a velcro surface are ideal and cut the lacquer crisply and quickly. During the initial stages of sanding keep taking lacquer off the print, not off the background. There should be only 2 or 3 coats of lacquer on the cut-outs. If there are more than this, the print will look 'buried'. Cut-outs and prints must be level with the background so the whole surface looks hand-painted.

It is necessary to place a towel across your legs to protect clothes. One side of the towel can be used to wipe any dust from the egg and the other side for wiping the block free of dust. It is important to keep both the sandpaper and the surface clean. Sanding is best done outdoors if possible to avoid irritation from dust. After each sanding is finished, wipe work with a damp lint-free cloth.

3. Apply 8 or 9 even dips.

4. Remove the stick with a sharp flexible blade by cutting through the lacquer on the stick about 6 mm down from the base of the egg. Do not cut the stick, just the lacquer. The stick will pull out leaving a small funnel of lacquer. Trim this off with the blade, but not too close to the egg. Let the sanding block take care of the final bit of lacquer. The dust will not settle on the egg during lacquering, so the major sand is just to level the surface of the cut-outs and the background. The final dip (which is executed in the same manner as the first dip) will leave a good finish. The final finish must be level and smooth. The final finish will never be perfect if the major sand is not properly done. Care is necessary not to create a water-wave effect from hard uneven sanding.

5. Place work aside for 2-3 weeks in a cool airy place to allow final coats to cure and harden. A micro-mesh final finish can be achieved using No. 4000-1200 sandpapers for a more professional appearance. Follow the instructions for use that come with the micro-mesh kit for use in decoupage work.

6. The hole is sealed with a tiny cut-out that matches the design. It is secured in place with a strong PVA glue. With a 00 brush, drop a little sealer onto the tiny cut-out. Allow to thoroughly dry. Repeat the process with lacquer. Allow to dry. The egg is now completely and safely sealed off from moisture.

FOLK ART

DESIGNED AND MADE BY KATE COOMBE
AND SANDRA GRIEVES

Folk Art originated with people interested in decorating their homes. Peasant folk, mostly farmers, started the artform, in the sixteenth or seventeenth century. The German word Bauernmalerai, meaning 'farm painting', gives some idea of the style of the work. The peasants who originally painted in this way had no formal training, and their techniques were passed down from one generation to another.

There are many styles of Folk Art with traditional techniques of design and colour. Different styles are associated with different countries. Designs can be simple with floral, scenic, animal or religious themes and it is said that anyone can learn simple folk art techniques.

Waratah Egg

REQUIREMENTS

sealer (Jo Sonja brand acrylic sealer was used for this egg)

paints (Jo Sonja brand acrylic paints were used for this egg)

Colours (Black, Titanium White, Green Oxide, Teal Green, Moss Green, Napthol Red Light, Burnt Umber, Vermillion, Yellow Oxide)

paint brushes (No 5 round brush, No 2 round brush, No 2 flat brush, No 4 flat brush, fine liner brush, small shader brush)

blown egg

stylus

varnish (water-based)

METHOD

1. Add a few drops of sealer to a small quantity of Black paint. Mix well. Using a No 5 round brush apply 2 coats to egg. Allow time to thoroughly dry between coats and after second coat.

2. Mix a little water with some Titanium White to form a transparent white. Using a No 4 flat brush and the transparent white paint, paint scallops around centre of egg. Using a stylus and a small amount of white paint, position dots around scallops.

3. Using a No 2 round brush and Green Oxide paint, paint leaves.

Allow to thoroughly dry. Tip a No 2 flat brush in Teal Green paint and blend to create shading as desired. Allow to thoroughly dry. Add a small quantity of water to a little Jade Green paint and paint veins on leaves using a fine liner brush.

4. Using a No 2 round brush, and White paint, create shape of waratah. Allow to thoroughly dry. Paint waratah in 2-3 coats Napthol Red Light paint. Allow to thoroughly dry. Using a No 2 round brush and Burnt Umber paint, paint small comma strokes down one side of waratah. Paint small Vermilion comma strokes down other side of waratah. Using a No 2 round brush and a mix of Vermilion and White apply small comma strokes to petals of waratah. Using a No 2 flat brush and Burnt Umber, shade in veins in centres of petals.

5. Flannel flowers are painted using a No 2 round brush and white paint. Allow to thoroughly dry. Create shading on each petal by loading brush with some White and pull through Moss Green on right side of brush. Stroke twice on each petal going in a clockwise direction. Allow to thoroughly dry. Stipple in centres using White, adding a little Moss Green shade around centre of flower. Allow to thoroughly dry. Stems are painted with a liner brush and Green Oxide paint. Allow

to thoroughly dry. Using a liner brush and White paint, paint in fern around waratah. Allow to thoroughly dry.

6. Using a No 5 round brush, seal by applying 2-3 coats of varnish, allowing to dry thoroughly between coats.

Country Scene Egg

REQUIREMENTS

paints (Jo Sonja brand paints were used for this egg)

Colours (Ultra Blue Deep, Titanium White, Jade Green, Black, Nimbus Grey, Green Oxide, Teal Green, Turner's Yellow,)

blown egg

paint brushes (No 4 round brush, shader brush, fine liner brush)

sealer (Jo Sonja brand sealer was used for this egg)

varnish (water-based)

METHOD

1. Mix a little Ultra Blue Deep and Titanium White to make 2 shades of blue. Using a No 4 round brush, paint top two thirds of egg as desired. Allow to dry. Create shading as desired with a second coat of paint. Allow to dry thoroughly. Add a little sealer to some watered down White paint. Using a shader brush, create white clouds on darker blue areas.

2. Using No 4 round brush and Jade green paint, create grass

across bottom third of egg. Allow to dry thoroughly. Using a liner brush and Black paint, position fence on start of grass.

3. Position trees on grass. Using a liner brush, and a mixture of Black, Nimbus Grey and Titanium white paints, paint in tree trunks and branches. Allow to dry thoroughly. Using a No 4 round brush and Jade green, Green oxide and Turner's yellow apply random clumps for leaves of trees.

4. Using a liner brush and some watered down Green Oxide paint, paint grass under trees. Allow to dry thoroughly. Using a liner brush and some watered down black paint, paint a few lines on top of green leaves on trees. Allow to dry thoroughly.

5. Using a No 5 round brush, seal by applying 2-3 coats of varnish, allowing to dry thoroughly between coats.

Large Cottage Garden Egg

REQUIREMENTS

JO SONJA ARTISTS ACRYLICS
Warm White, Plum Pink, Ultra Blue Deep, Turner's Yellow, Burgundy, Sapphire, Vermillion, Red Earth, Teal Green, Moss Greengreen, Oxide Black

OTHER MATERIALS
Wooden Egg
7mm (¼") masking tape
Sea Sponge
No 3 round brush
No 2 flat brush
Liner brush

PREPARATION
Basecoat the egg with several coats of Warm White so that it is all white. When the egg is completely dry, place strips of 7 mm (¼") masking tape in a criss-cross pat-

tern from the top of the egg (that is, the pointed end) to about half way down the sides.

Using a mix of Teal Green, Green Oxide and Moss Green on the sea sponge, sponge the egg about two-thirds up from the base. Turn the sponge constantly so that there is a mix of greens but with more Teal towards the bottom. Sponge all over the egg including the masking tape and allow to dry. Remove the masking tape and re-sponge with some mixed green over the edges of the tape and a little up towards the top.

PROCEDURE

1. HOLLYHOCKS

Using the liner brush and some thinned down Green Oxide, paint in a series of wavy lines from the top of the sponging to the base of the egg. Change to the round brush and Plum Pink and paint the hollyhock blossoms all down the green wavy stems. When these are dry, sideload the flat brush with Burgundy and float a centre-circle in all the front-on flowers. Those blossoms you wish to be 'side-on', float a wavy line across the centre with the Burgundy to the inside.

2. LAVENDER

Mix a silvery green from Green Oxide, Warm White and Black. Turn the egg upside down and paint a series of 'umbrella spines' for stems with the liner brush and the silvery green. They need to start below the hollyhocks but

reach up into the flowers. As with an umbrella, the stems need to join at the base.

Mix a few shades of lavender from Plum Pink and Ultramarine or Burgundy and Ultramarine with White. Using the liner brush, load these mixes with a little extra White here and there, and bounce small sideways half-commas up each of the stalks. Allow the colours to 'brush-mix' and become smaller and smaller as they reach the top of the stem.

3. DAFFODILS

Using Turners Yellow and a No 3 round brush, paint short fat comma strokes in a five-stroke star pattern and in a staggered line over the base of the lavender bushes. Mix some Vermillion with the Turner's Yellow to make a light orange and base in a circle of this colour in the centre of the star pattern.

When this is dry, change to the liner brush and with a mix of Vermillion and Burgundy paint a wriggly line around the light orange circle. The sideways daffodils have the light orange circle painted on one side of the yellow petals and the wriggly line is an oval on the outside end of the light orange circle. The stems and leaves are a light yellow green made by mixing Turner's Yellow and Green Oxide.

4. FORGET-ME-NOTS

With the liner brush double-loaded in Sapphire and White, place 'push-dab' clusters of little flowers all around the base of the egg. Use them to cover the base of the stems of the daffodils and the lavender. Try as much as possible to keep them in five petal sets, then place a dot of Turner's Yellow in the centre of each or, if you feel up to it, a double-load push-dab dot of Turner's Yellow sideloaded with Red Earth.

FINISHING

When the painting is completely dry and has had a few days to cure, varnish with several coats of clear satin or gloss varnish.

Berry Egg

PALETTE

Teal Green, Raw Sienna, Burgundy, Green Oxide, Turner's Yellow, Napthol Red Light, Moss Green, Warm White, Black, Jade Green, Pine Green, Storm Blue

OTHER MATERIALS

Wooden egg
No 2 flat brush
No 3 round brush
Liner brush

PREPARATION

Basecoat the egg with several coats of Teal Green. Allow to dry thoroughly.

PROCEDURE

1. LEAVES

Using a No 3 round brush, stroke in a layer of black leaves from the base of the egg to about three-quarters of the way up the sides. Make them overlap at the base and spread out at the top. At the top include some berries on stems. Make the berries using the handle of the brush dipped in the black paint to make a dot then join these to the leaves with the liner brush stems.

Over the black, paint a layer of large leaves in Green Oxide coming to just below the black leaves and outlined in Moss Green. Next, if there is room, paint a scattered layer of ivy leaves (three comma strokes with their round ends overlapping) in jade, outlined in Raw Sienna. A final layer of leaves can be the ferns which are a series of tiny comma strokes in a double row (as though on a stem)

in a light blue made with Storm Blue, White and a touch of Moss Green.

2. STRAWBERRIES

Basecoat the strawberries in Warm White with enough coats to cover the background. When these are completely dry, paint the fruit with at least two coats of Napthol Red Light. Shade each strawberry with the round brush loaded first with Napthol Red Light and a sideload of Burgundy. Paint a shape-following stroke on the same side of each strawberry so the Burgundy is on the outside and blends into the Napthol Red Light on the centre of each fruit. Repeat this process for the highlight on the other side of the berry using Turner's Yellow instead of Burgundy. Stroke in the tiny Black seeds with the tip of the liner brush, then on the highlight side of the seeds on the highlighted half of the strawberry place an even smaller stroke of White. Drybrush some white high-

lights on the yellow side of the strawberries, then with the liner brush loaded in teal Green stroke in the long wavy sepals to make the cap on each strawberry.

3. RASPBERRIES

Basecoat the berries in enough coats of Warm White to cover the background then paint with at least two coats of Burgundy and allow to dry. Float a highlight of Napthol Red Light on each nodule of the raspberries, then outline them with a fine line in a pink made from Burgundy and White. Highlight each one with a drybrush comma in White. The raspberry sepal caps are Pine Green sideloaded with Moss Green.

Grape Egg

PALETTE

Red Earth, Black, Yellow Oxide, Burgundy, Green Oxide, Gold Oxide, Storm Blue, Jade, Warm White, French Blue

OTHER MATERIALS

Wooden egg
No 2 flat brush
No 3 round brush
Liner brush

PREPARATION

Basecoat the egg in at least two or more coats of Red Earth. Allow to Dry.

PROCEDURE

1. LEAVES

With a No 3 round brush stroke in a layer of Black leaves overlapping at the base and spreading out at the top which should be about three quarters of the way up the egg. At the top place some berries in black, using the handle of the brush dipped in paint, and join them to the leaves with some fine stems.

Over this stroke in some large leaves in Green Oxide outlined with Moss Green. Then paint some ivy leaves in another layer with Jade Green and an outline of Gold Oxide. The fern leaves are Yellow Oxide and are painted around and between the other leaves.

2. GRAPES

The Red, Purple and Blue Grapes are all painted the same way so I will just give one set of instructions and the colour mixes and you just repeat the process.

Dark Blue = French Blue,

Medium Blue = French Blue + White + Yellow Oxide 1:2:.05,

Light Blue = Medium Blue + White.

Dark Red = Burgundy,

Medium Red = Burgundy + White + Yellow Oxide 1:2:.05,

Light Red = Medium Red + White.

Dark Purple = Ultramarine + burgundy + white 1:1:.05,

Medium Purple = Dark Purple + White,

Light Purple = Medium Purple + White.

Basecoat one third of the grapes in the dark hue and shade these in a darker colour. (Storm Blue, Burgundy mixed with a little Black, or Ultramarine). Basecoat the next third of the grapes in the medium hue overlapping and interspersed with the previous layer. Shade these with the dark colour of the previous basecoat and highlight them with the Light Blue, Red and Purple. The final third of each bunch of grapes are painted in the lightest hue, shaded with the medium or dark colour (whichever you feel gives the most contrast) then highlighted with drybrushed white. Try to shade all the grapes on the same side and then highlight them on the opposite side to the shading.

Finally, with Black on the liner brush paint in some small stalks on the lightest or uppermost grapes.

Simpler Ideas

DYEING EGGS

A wide range of products can be purchased from craft suppliers to decorate eggs. Dyes for colouring eggs can be obtained by using a wide variety of mediums. Follow the instructions on the packet for the preparation of commercial dyestuffs.

Crepe paper can be used to add to water to make a simple dye bath.

Vegetables such as onions, spinach and beet can be used to make dye to colour eggs at home. These vegetables can all be prepared according to the directions for the Onion Skin Dye. The onion will give a yellow dye, the spinach a light green dye and the beet a reddish colour. The amount of vegetable used will depend on the shade you require.

Strong tea made from ordinary or herbal teas will provide a range of colours.

Onion Skin Dye

One of the oldest and most effective dyes can be obtained by using the outer skins of brown onions.

REQUIREMENTS
20 (approx) large brown onions
cold water
1 tablespoon brown vinegar (to 'fix' dye — make it more permanent)

METHOD
1. Peel outer skin from onions.
2. Place skins into a large saucepan.
3. Cover with cold water.
4. Bring to the boil with the lid on. Allow to simmer for 10 minutes.
4. Strain the liquid dye and discard the skins.
5. Add vinegar and stir well.
6. Allow dye to cool completely.
7. Place hard-boiled eggs into cold dye. Bring slowly to the boil.
8. Simmer for approx. 10 minutes or until egg has taken on the colour required.
9. Dry eggs completely before decorating as desired.

Decorated Eggs

1. Paints used for these eggs are acrylic craft paints. Folk Art paints are also suitable to use. Best results are obtained if the egg is painted all at once. If the egg is painted in two separate steps a line may appear. Carefully hold the egg at the ends with the finger tips when painting it. To dry the egg, carefully balance the narrow pointed end into the dimple of an egg carton. When applying more than one coat of paint, allow each coat to dry thoroughly before applying the next coat.

2. Eggs must be completely immersed in dye to obtain an even shade.

3. Glue used is PVA hobby glue. A fine paint brush or a toothpick can be used to apply glue. The advantage of using a toothpick is it can be discarded after use.

4. Good quality fine paint brushes must be used.

5. Sealer used is a craft sealer. Artwork sealer is also suitable. Clear Estapol in matt or gloss may also be used.

Paint, glue, paint brushes and sealer can be obtained from craft suppliers.

Glitter Egg

REQUIREMENTS

acrylic paint
blown egg
craft glue
glitter
No 5 round brush
braid
old egg carton

METHOD

1. Apply 2 coats of paint to egg, allowing time to dry between coats and after second coat.

2. Coat the rounded end half of the painted egg with glue. Take care to leave a 5 mm (³⁄₁₆") band around the centre of the egg without any glue. This is left for a smooth surface on which to stick the braid.

3. Sprinkle glitter over glue on egg.

4. Carefully balance egg in the dimple of an egg carton and allow to dry.

5. Repeat steps 2-4 with the other half of the egg.

6. Brush around centre of egg with glue. Place braid around egg and press gently but firmly into position. Carefully balance egg in the dimple of an egg carton to dry.

Dried Flower Egg

Small, rather than large, dried flowers and ferns are best for decorating eggs. Flowers must be thoroughly dried before use.

REQUIREMENTS

acrylic paint

blown egg

No 5 round brush

craft glue

tweezers

dried flowers

narrow ribbon

sealer (Spray sealer can be obtained from craft shops.)

METHOD

1. Apply 2 coats of paint to egg, allowing time to dry between coats and after second coat.

2. Brush back of flowers with glue.

3. Using tweezers, arrange flowers in the desired pattern. Allow glue to dry.

4. Finish with a narrow knotted ribbon.

5. To preserve decoration, carefully apply spray sealer.

Pressed Flower Egg

REQUIREMENTS

sealer

paint (Jo Sonja brand paint was used for this egg.) Colour — Rich Gold

No 5 round brush, No 4 round brush

blown egg

small pressed flower and pressed leaves

craft glue

varnish (spray varnish)

METHOD

1. Add a couple of drops of sealer to a little Rich Gold paint. Mix well. Using a No 5 round brush apply 2 coats of paint over egg. Allow to thoroughly dry betwen coats.

2. Using a No 4 round brush apply a little glue to egg. Carefully arrange flowers and leaves as desired.

3. Seal by spraying with 2-3 coats of varnish, allowing to thoroughly dry between coats.

Paper Cut-out Egg

REQUIREMENTS

acrylic paint

No 5 round brush

blown egg

fine nail scissors

gift wrapping paper

craft glue

sealer

METHOD

1. Apply 2 coats of paint to egg, allowing time to dry between coats and after second coat.

2. Using a fine pair of nail scissors, very carefully cut out a selection of small patterns from gift-wrapping paper.

3. Apply glue liberally to reverse side of cut-out shapes. (It does not matter if a little glue gets on the correct side of the paper cut-outs.)

4. Carefully arrange shapes to form desired patterns. Allow to completely dry.

5. Apply 2-3 coats of sealer, allowing drying time between coats.

Beaded Egg

REQUIREMENTS

acrylic paint

No 5 round brush

blown egg

craft glue

tweezers

beads

sealer

METHOD

1. Apply 2 coats of paint to egg, allowing time to dry between coats and after second coat.

2. Apply glue to back of beads.

3. Using tweezers, carefully arrange beads on egg. Allow to completely dry.

4. Apply 2-3 coats of sealer, allowing drying time between coats.

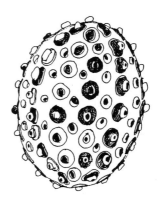

Icing Flowers

Small icing flowers and leaves can be used to decorate eggs. These can be made at home or purchased from specialist cake icing shops. If you wish to make icing flowers at home, refer to a specialist cake icing book for instructions for making and shaping.

REQUIREMENTS

icing flowers and leaves

acrylic paint

No 5 round brush

blown egg

craft glue

spray sealer

METHOD

1. Apply 2 coats of paint to egg, allowing time to dry between coats and after second coat.

2. Apply a little glue to decorations and carefully arrange decorations on egg.

3. Allow to dry for several hours.

4. Carefully apply 2-3 coats of sealer, allowing drying time between coats.

Batik

It is a good idea to practice working with wax on paper before you commence on an egg. For lasting results it is best to work on blown eggs.

Batik is a Javanese word. It is a wax resistant technique of pattern dyeing. The parts of the egg not required to take the dye are covered with hot wax, after which the egg is dipped into a dye bath.

REQUIREMENTS

straight pins (select heads of various sizes)

large cork (to stick pins in when not in use)

feather quills

one potato (cut in half)

2 old spoons

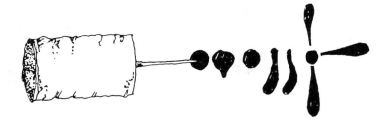

large round (5 cm, ³⁄₁₆") candle stub

wax (equal parts of paraffin and beeswax)

old cups for prepared dye

soft absorbent cloth

blown eggs

dye bath (Select type and colours as desired and make up according to the given directions for each dye. Prepare a strong dye bath, as this helps to avoid wax melting if the egg is left in the dye bath for too long.)

old egg carton

METHOD

1. Bend the handle of the old spoon and secure it into half a potato. Place a small amount of prepared wax in the bowl of the spoon. Set up according to illustration.

2. Arrange spoon so that it sits over the candle flame. Heat wax with candle flame until melted. Do not allow wax to boil in spoon.

3. Dip a pin head into melted wax and touch the surface of the egg shell very quickly to make a dot of wax. Tear shapes can be made with melted wax by drawing the pin along the egg shell. The pin head must be dipped into the hot wax for each dot or shape. Only a very small amount of wax will stick to the pin each time.

4. Larger shapes can be created by using the tips of quills using the same method as for the pins.

5. When eggs have been completely decorated as desired with wax designs, allow to dry completely by balancing in the dimple of an egg carton.

6. Carefully place each egg into prepared dye bath. The dye must be warm in order for the shell to take the dye evenly. If the dye is too hot (above 280°C), it will melt the wax. Carefully turn egg in dye for

approx. 1 minute. When the desired shade is reached, carefully remove egg with another old spoon and place on the dimple of an egg carton to dry.

7. If only one shade is required, wax can be removed. This can be done by holding the egg near the side of a candle flame. (Do not use the tip of the flame as soot will form on the egg.) Using a soft absorbent cloth, carefully soak up wax as it melts. Do not remove wax by scratching as the design may be spoiled.

8. When additional colours are required, the wax is left on after the first dye bath. When the egg is completely dry add more wax designs.

9. Dye eggs again in a stronger colour dye bath.

10. Repeat steps 8 and 9 again up to five (5) times in total, as desired. Remember to work from a lighter up to a darker colour. A helpful guide is to start with white and progress through yellow, orange, light red, dark red, blue, violet to black.

11. Remember the wax is only removed after the final dye bath is completed.

Waxing

This method is different from Batik (as seen on page 72) as the wax remains on the finished work of art.

It is necessary to use pure beeswax as it is pliable and may be flattened into thin layers and then cut into shapes as desired and attached to the surface of the egg. Melted wax instead of craft glue is used to attach the wax patterns to the egg.

Variations of this can be carried out by using melted coloured wax and applying it in the method of Batik (see page 72). Remember this time the wax remains permanently on the egg.

Natural or dyed eggs can be used for waxing.

Scratching

Scratching requires a very steady hand and a lot of patience. One egg can take up to one hour to scratch. The end result is worth the time if you enjoy this form of craft.

Blown eggs can be used for this technique if they are handled very carefully. Hard-boiled eggs are best used as they are less fragile.

REQUIREMENTS

hard-boiled egg (eggs with a thick, smooth shell are best)

dye bath

metal instruments (eg. pins, needles, nailfile, penknife, razor blade, paring knife, fine tools etc.)

wax crayons

soft cloth

floor wax, clear Estapol, or colourless fingernail polish (to coat finished eggs)

METHOD

1. Dye hard-boiled egg according to directions on dye. Allow to completely dry.

2. Using a metal instrument of your choice scratch a design

into the dyed surface of the egg. Best results for beginners can be obtained by partitioning the egg. Designs can then be worked within these partitioned areas.

3. More colourful effects can be obtained with the scratch tech-

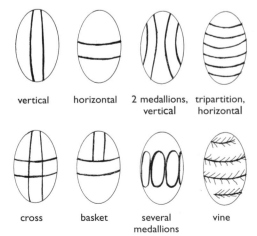

vertical   horizontal   2 medallions,   tripartition,
                          vertical   horizontal

cross   basket   several   vine
                   medallions

nique by first colouring the egg, (while it is still warm) with wax crayons. Several layers of crayon in various colours can be used, progressing from light to dark colour. Depending on how deep you scratch, the design will appear in various colours. This process is much easier for younger children as it is less tedious, because wax crayon is much more easily scratched away. The colours of the wax crayon stay on the egg surface, while dyes penetrate the shell. After using wax crayons, hold the eggs in a soft cloth as you work, to avoid crayons smudging.

VARIATION

This variation is worked on blown eggs.

REQUIREMENTS

blown egg

dye bath

knitting needle

wax (equal parts of paraffin and beeswax mixed with crayon to obtain desired colour)

sharp tool

METHOD

1. Dye blown egg according to directions on dye. Allow to completely dry.

2. Carefully poke a knitting needle through the holes that were used to blow the egg.

3. Carefully dip egg into melted coloured wax.

4. Secure ends of needle to allow egg to dry.

5. When wax is completely firm, use a sharp tool and carefully scratch or cut away wax (depending on thickness of wax) to form designs in the surface.

6. Coat egg with several coats of sealer, allowing drying time between coats.

Blocking

Small flowers, grasses, fresh herbs, small leaves, paper or fabric cut-outs can be used to make pattern blocks on eggs. Pattern blocks are arranged on eggs and secured with a tight stocking. Eggs are dyed to the desired shade, and then hung to dry. When the pattern block is removed, the imprint of the pattern remains. Non colour-fast blocks can be used for desired effects. These will allow some of the dye to penetrate the pattern and the imprint will be in a paler shade than the rest of the egg.

REQUIREMENTS

blown eggs

small flowers etc

egg white, salad oil or vegetable glue (to stick block onto egg) Do not use craft glues as these react with dyes.

old stocking or fine muslin cloth

thread (to secure stocking)

dye bath (make up dye according to directions)

oil or sealer

METHOD

1. Make sure surface of egg is completely clean and free from grease.

2. Brush the reverse side of block pattern etc. with a thin smear of vegetable oil or egg white.

3. Arrange design with pattern block(s), with reverse side of pattern onto egg.

4. Carefully wrap egg in a single layer of old stocking. Tie stocking securely at both ends with strong thread. Make sure the stocking is pulled tightly over the egg to ensure the pattern

block(s) remain in place during dyeing.

5. Immerse egg into dye bath. Bring slowly to the boil and simmer for 10 minutes. If a darker shade of dye is required, leave egg in dye until liquid cools.

6. Remove egg from dye and hang up to dry, leaving until all the moisture has run out of the stocking, but it is not completely dry. If it is left until completely dry, it may be difficult to remove pattern block(s) from egg.

7. When completely dry, rub over with a little oil or apply 2-3 coats of sealer, allowing drying time between coats.

Appliqué

Small pieces of lace, ribbon, felt, paper, fabric, wax, straw, leaves, metal or almost any medium that you desire can be glued onto an egg. Almost all of these items can be found around the home or purchased from craft suppliers.

Straw Appliqué

The straw for this form of craft must be resilient and not brittle or dry. Do not try to flatten straw with an iron.

The craft is very tedious and time consuming and is not recommended for impatient children. The end results from many hours of work are very rewarding.

REQUIREMENTS

fine natural straw
shape knife
blunt knife-blade
dyed blown egg
craft glue
sealer

METHOD

1. Soak straw in warm water for approx. 20 minutes to soften.

2. Slit each piece of straw and flatten it on the inside with a blunt knife-blade. As soon as the ends of the straw begin to curl, cut it into shapes (strips, squares, triangles and/or diamonds as desired).

3. Place a small amount of glue onto dull side of straw and position it onto egg. Use a fine needle or pin to help position straw.

4. When design work is completed allow to dry completely.

5. Seal as desired.

Ribbon, Lace and Braid Appliqué

This method of design can be very simple or ornate as desired. Trimmings of your choice can be used. Ribbon, lace and/or coloured braids make very attractive craft work.

REQUIREMENTS

trimmings
blown egg
craft glue
sealer

METHOD

1. Apply trimmings to egg using craft glue. Allow glue to completely dry.

2. Seal as desired.

YARN

A variety of brightly coloured yarns can be used to decorate eggs. More than one colour can be used on each egg. Experimentation can be carried out with a variety of different textures. Yarn can be wound around egg in wavy lines or patterns as desired.

Yarn has been used to decorate eggs in Poland for many years. It originated with the use of a marrow-like substance obtained from rushes. This was applied to the egg. It was responsible for the inspiration of the use of yarn to decorate eggs.

REQUIREMENTS

yarn
craft glue
blown egg
old egg carton
sealer

METHOD

1. Apply glue to one half of the egg.
2. Arrange yarn as desired around egg. Tuck the end of the yarn into the small hole left from blowing the egg.
3. Balance in the dimple of an egg carton and allow to dry.
4. Repeat steps 1-3 for other half of egg, tucking the end of the yarn in the hole at the other end of the egg.
5. Seal as desired.

Other creative work

- Simple designs on eggs can be made by cutting patterns out from masking tape and sticking it onto the eggs before dyeing. It is important to allow the eggs to cool and dry completely after dyeing, before removing the tape.

- Crayons can be used to draw on eggs before they are dyed. The area covered with crayon will not absorb the dye.
- Ordinary water colour paints can be used by children to paint dyed eggs. These make a very simple and attractive gift for a friend.
- Finished works of art can be given a coat of varnish (Estapol) in either a matt or gloss finish. This will preserve the art-work and the egg. For ease of handling, coat the top half of the egg with varnish and place the un-varnished part into an egg carton to dry completely. Repeat the process with the other half.
- Unvarnished, finished eggs can be given a quick gloss by rubbing with a little vegetable oil.

Ideas for Children

Through many years of experience of teaching craft to children, I have seen evidence of the immense fun children derive from decorating their own eggs.

Methods used should be aimed at the level of ability of the children involved. If the craft is too complicated, children will become frustrated. If it is too simple, idle hands will create their own crafty ideas!

When children are allowed to create their own works of art, they have a self-motivated expression that has no preconceived adult ideas. Children should be allowed to express their own creativity with only enough adult stimulation to motivate the concept.

The physical stimulation of creating colour, shape and texture around an egg can be very rewarding for the child. The sense of touch for the young child as they work with paint is very relaxing. Abstract concepts of reality can be developed within the child's ability to produce works of art.

The following ideas may be of help to those working with children.

Finger painting

To help children explore the concept of decorating eggs, finger painting is a good way to begin.

REQUIREMENTS

finger paints
hard-boiled eggs
old egg carton
sealer

METHOD

1. Apply finger paint to egg.
2. Allow egg to completely dry by balancing in the dimple of an egg carton.
3. Seal as desired.

Potato Prints

Printing blocks can be inexpensively prepared by working with potato cut-outs.

Suggest to children that they do not make their potato-blocks larger than 1 cm (⅜") or they will not obtain a good impression on the rounded surface of eggs. See shapes on page 82 for ideas for patterns.

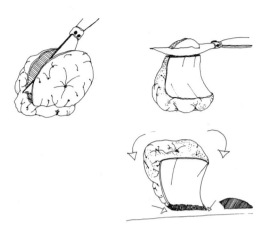

2. Using a large brush apply poster paint to potato blocks.

3. Decorate eggs with patterns as desired.

4. If more than one colour is used, eggs must be allowed to dry in between each colour. It may be easier for children to manage if only half the egg is decorated at a time and allowed to dry.

REQUIREMENTS

sharp knife

potatoes

large paint brush

poster paints

hard-boiled eggs

egg carton

METHOD

1. Using a sharp knife cut out printing blocks in potatoes.

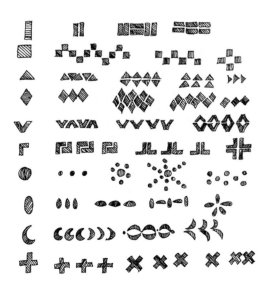

Transfers

Transfers are a great idea for children to use to decorate eggs. Less pressure is necessary to be able to display creative talents. Children can take part in this form of decoration using small Easter egg transfers. Additional transfers of small patterns can be added to make a variety of finished eggs. Children can derive a great deal of joy in seeing their finished works of art without necessarily experiencing advanced craft.

Blown eggs are more durable while hard-boiled eggs are more substantial to work on. The person decorating the eggs can decide which they prefer to use. The age of the children will be a factor in deciding this.

Requirements

eggs (blown or hard-boiled, natural or dyed as desired)

transfers

sealer

METHOD

1. Make sure eggs are completely clean and dry and free of grease.
2. Apply transfers as desired following directions for their use.
3. Seal as desired.

Paper Cut-outs

This is another excellent idea for young children. Coloured gummed stickers are excellent to use. Small shapes can be purchased and used to make patterns. Larger stickers can be cut into shapes as desired.

REQUIREMENTS

gummed stickers
hard-boiled eggs
sealer

METHOD

1. Arrange stickers onto egg in desired pattern.
2. Seal as desired.

Paper Mosaic

This is another easy idea for children to work with. Paper can be torn into small pieces and arranged in an abstract design or cut into shapes and arranged in a geometric design.

REQUIREMENTS

coloured paper
craft glue
hard-boiled eggs
sealer

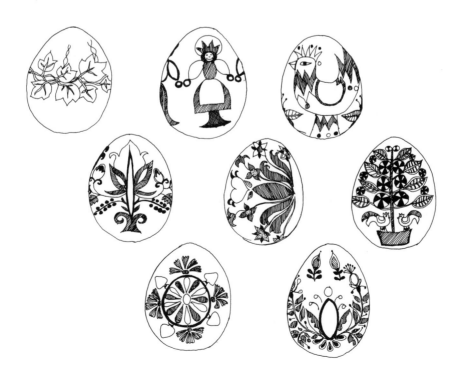

METHOD

1. Tear or cut paper into small pieces.
2. Apply glue to reverse side of paper.
3. Arrange on egg in desired pattern.
4. Seal as desired.

Batik for children

Refer to the instructions for working with Batik on page 71.

This simplified technique for batik can be used by children.

It is necessary to supervise small children while they are working with a burning candle!

REQUIREMENTS

candle
hard-boiled eggs
dye bath

METHOD

1. Allow wax to drip from a burning candle onto the egg. Small drops of wax can form dots on the egg. The wax can be allowed to run around the egg by turning the egg slowly as the wax drips onto the egg. Streaks can be made by doing this. When design work is finished, allow wax to completely harden.
2. Dye eggs as desired.
3. Repeat steps 1 & 2 several times, with different colours of dye. Refer to page 72 for method of dyeing batik eggs.

Remember not to remove any wax until all the work is completed. Refer to page 74 for method of removing wax from eggs.

Wax Dipping

REQUIREMENTS

wax crayons
candle
old spoon
potato (cut in half)
dyed or natural hard-boiled eggs
soft cloth
old egg carton

METHOD

1. Follow points 1 & 2 in the method of setting up as for Batik on page 73 to melt wax crayons.
2. Several wax colours many be used on the one egg. The colours of the wax crayon stay on the egg surface. After using wax crayons, hold the egg in a soft cloth as you work, to avoid crayons smudging.
3. When eggs have been com-

pletely decorated as desired with wax designs, allow to dry completely by balancing in the dimple of an egg carton. When additional colours are required, make sure each colour of wax is completely dry before adding more wax.

Poster paints

Using poster paints or water colours is a very simple medium for children to use.

REQUIREMENTS

poster paints
paint brushes
hard-boiled dyed or natural eggs
old egg carton
sealer

METHOD

1. Using poster paints and paint brushes of desired sizes make patterns onto egg. It may be easiest to paint egg one half at a time and dry in the dimple of an egg carton. Allow to dry completely.
2. Seal as desired.

Felt-tip Pens

This is possibly the easiest form of decorating eggs. Most children can manage this technique.

REQUIREMENTS

felt tip pens (water resistant)
hard-boiled dyed or natural eggs
sealer

METHOD

1. Draw patterns on eggs as desired with felt tipped pens. Lots of ideas are included on pages 86-87.
2. Seal as desired.

Herb Heads

This is a very effective way of decorating your kitchen window sill over Easter. Herbs are grown in egg shells.

Seeds should sprout in a couple of days. It is essential to keep the top layer of cotton wool moistened at all time. The top layer of cotton wool is removed when spouts appear. This will allow the sprouts to get air and stand upright. Keep moistened during growth.

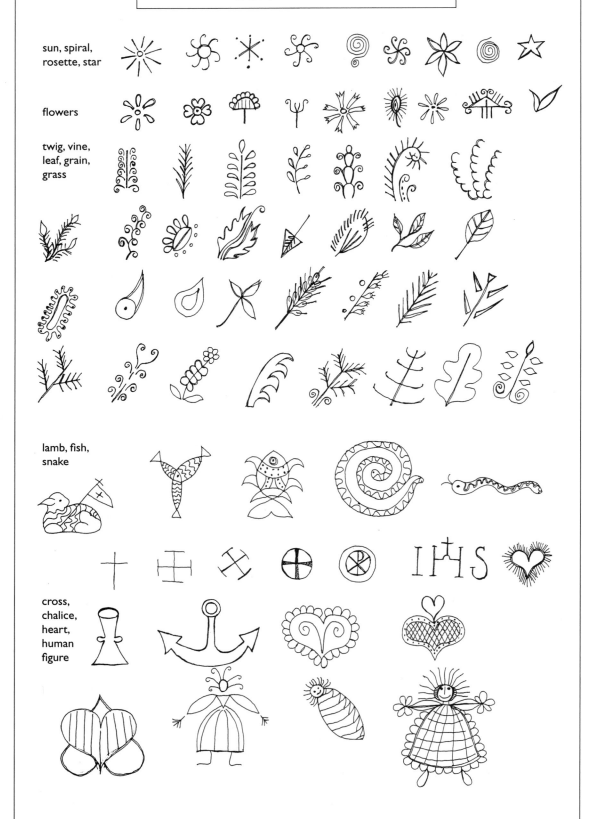

sun, spiral, rosette, star

flowers

twig, vine, leaf, grain, grass

lamb, fish, snake

cross, chalice, heart, human figure

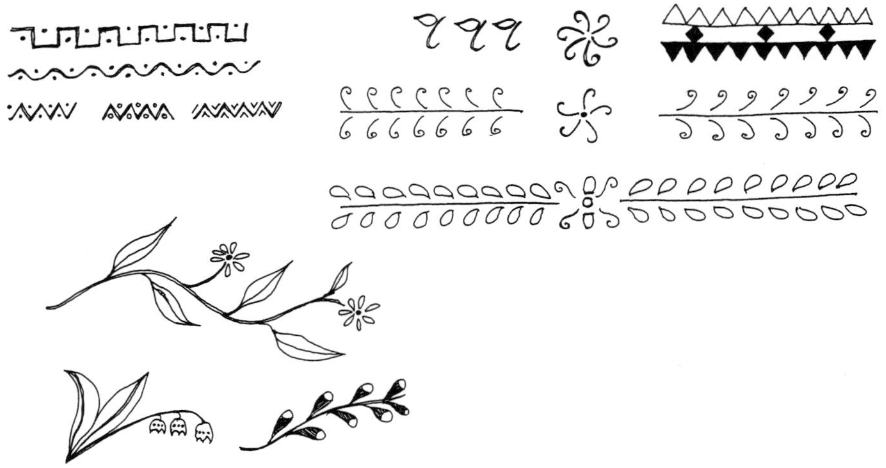

line

dash

dot

shuttle, haying
fork, rake, cradle,
bird house

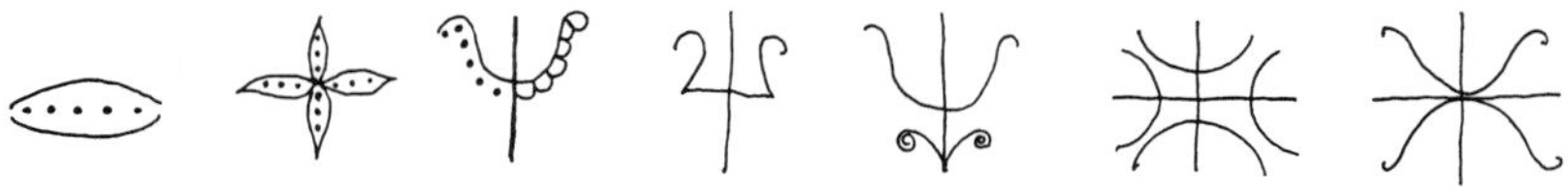

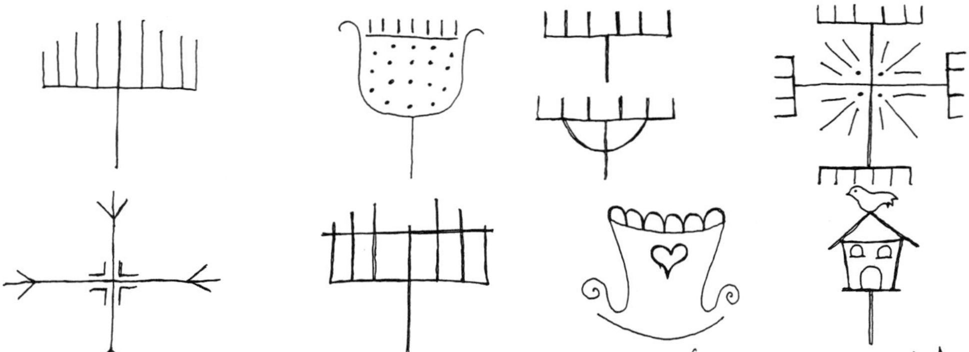

bird, chicken,
rooster

When Easter is over and the window-sill decoration is no longer required, take shells from egg cups and carefully break shells away from cotton wool. Gently loosen cotton wool and place into soil to continue growing.

From this exercise, you have entertained the children and provided a window-sill decoration for Easter and produced a longer growing herb.

REQUIREMENTS

hard-boiled eggs

alfalfa or quick-growing seeds

cotton wool

felt-tipped pens and/or poster paints

egg cups

METHOD

1. Carefully and neatly cut top off egg. Carefully remove egg from inside shell. Remove as much egg as possible from shell taking care not break shell.

2. Decorate shells as desired and sit in an egg cup to dry. Take care not to put design on egg shell that will be lower than the top of the egg-cup. Shells are fragile and need careful handling.

3. Fill empty shell with cotton wool.

4. Sprinkle seeds onto cotton wool Moisten with water.

5. Cover with a thin layer of cotton wool. Moisten with water.

6. Place egg-cups on window sill.

7. Keep cotton wool moist.

Seeds should sprout in 5-7 days.

The Egg Tree

The egg tree originated in Germany many years ago. Today some people like to hang their decorated eggs onto a branch or small tree. Fine cord can be threaded through the finished decorated egg and the cord used to hang the egg on the tree. It is easier to thread blown eggs than hard-boiled eggs.

BIRCH BRANCHES

At Easter time, the Swedes decorate small birch branches with coloured feathers. In Australia, small eucalyptus branches can be used in place of birch branches.

REQUIREMENTS

coloured inks

feathers (these can be obtained from an old pillow)

paper towel

fine thread

small branches

METHOD

1. Using inks colour feathers. (Do not use paint as the feathers will become sticky.) Allow to completely dry on a paper towel.

2. Using thread, attach feathers to branch.

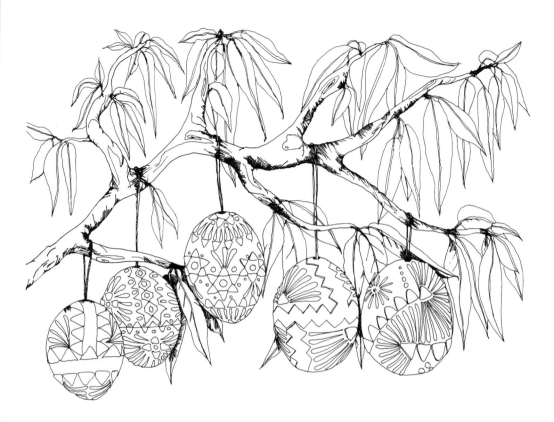

Easter Bonnets or Hats

In some schools or small towns, there is a contest for the best Easter bonnet worn in an Easter parade. Decorated eggs can be arranged around the brim of a hat.

TO MAKE A HAT

REQUIREMENTS

thin cardboard

staples

craft glue

poster paint

paint brush

METHOD

1. Cut a large strip of cardboard about 15 cm (6") wide.

2. Wrap cardboard around head. Tape or staple the cylinder together to fit head and keep shape.

3. Place cylinder on the centre of another piece of cardboard. Draw a circle around the outside of the cylinder.

4. Lift cylinder and cut out the circle you have just drawn. (The circle will be the top of the hat.)

5. Round the corners of the piece of cardboard from which you cut the circle. (This will become the brim.)

6. Cut 6 x 5 cm (2") slits in top and bottom of cylinder.

7. Slide cylinder through round opening in the brim. Fold bottom flaps out, and glue the brim to the flaps.

8. Fold the top flaps in. Glue the top in place.

9. Paint a bright design on your top hat. Glue on a feather if you wish.

10. Glue on decorated eggs around brim of hat.

TO MAKE A BONNET

REQUIREMENTS

1 x 30 cm (12") paper plate

scissors

wall-paper

craft glue

poster paints

brush

2 x 30 cm (12") ribbons

METHOD

1. Straighten one side of paper plate by drawing a 22.5 cm (9") line from edge to edge. Cut along line.

2. Cut 5 cm (2") slits all around the curved edge of the paper plate.

3. Fit a 30 cm (12") strip of wall-paper around curved edge. Fold flaps in, and glue wall-paper to flaps.

4. Poke holes though bottom two edges of paper. Attach a 30 cm (12") length of ribbon to each hole.

5. Paint and decorate as desired.

TO MAKE A BASKET

REQUIREMENTS

aluminium foil

container for mould of basket (eg. margarine container)

poster paint (some forms of paint will not adhere to foil. A little dishwashing detergent can be added in the proportion of 2 teaspoons to 1 cup paint.)

paint brushes

cord (for handles)

METHOD

1. Cover outside and inside of container with one large sheet of foil. Take care as foil tears easily. Trim excess foil and press firmly into shape.

2. Paint design onto foil. Allow to dry.

3. Staple cord to sides of basket to make handles. Large baskets will require 2 heavier cords for balancing.

GRASS BASKETS

Follow the above method for making a foil basket.

REQUIREMENTS

basket container

potting mixture

lawn seed

METHOD

1. Place approx. 3 cm of potting mixture into a basket you have made.

2. Sprinkle lawn seed thickly on top of mixture. Cover seeds with a thin layer of cotton wool. Moisten cotton wool.

3. Leave moistened cotton wool in place until shoots appear. Carefully remove cotton wool.

4. Continue to water seeds carefully.

Place grass basket on a light window-sill during growing.

Seeds are best sown approx. 3-4 weeks before Easter to allow grass to grow. When Easter time arrives, arrange decorated eggs in grass basket.

Yellow Easter Chick

REQUIREMENTS

1 egg
yellow dye
small piece of yellow paper
hobby glue
felt-tip pen

METHOD

1. Hard-boil egg and allow to cool completely.

2. Dye with yellow dye and allow to cool and dry completely.

3. Cut a beak, tail, pair of wings and two feet out of the yellow paper. Glue parts to the egg.

4. Using a felt-tip pen draw 2 eyes.

Yellow Chick in Decorated Egg Shell

The little yellow chick has found a home in this decorated egg shell.

REQUIREMENTS

large blown hen egg
fine pointed sharp scissors

Yellow Easter Chick

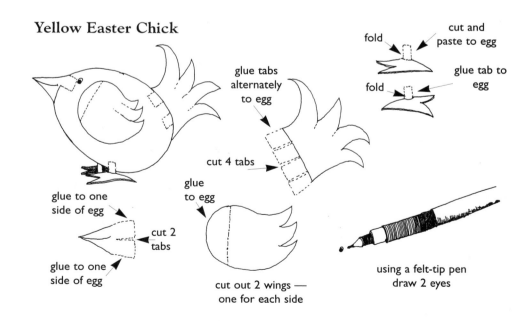

glue tabs alternately to egg

cut 4 tabs

cut and paste to egg

fold

glue tab to egg

fold

glue to one side of egg

cut 2 tabs

glue to one side of egg

glue to egg

cut out 2 wings — one for each side

using a felt-tip pen draw 2 eyes

few drops white vinegar in water to rinse inside of egg shell

10 cm (4") x 5 cm (2") x 1 cm (⅜") thick foam oasis for base

craft glue

several stalks of small dark green dried flowers

1 bunch small bright yellow dried flowers for inside of shell

tweezers

small quantity white dried daisies with yellow centres for edge of shell

small quantity yellow dried flowers to cover base

small quantity white dried flowers to cover base

spray lacquer

20 cm (8") x 1 cm (⅜") yellow satin ribbon to go around edge of foam base

15 cm (6") x 2 mm (¹⁄₁₀") yellow cord for bow

1 small yellow fluffy chicken for inside of egg

METHOD

1. Mark oval approx. 4 cm x 3 cm (³⁄₁₆" x ⅛") on egg shell (roughly ¼ surface of egg).

2. Using point of scissors, make a hole in the centre of the oval to be removed. Carefully cut out oval shape.

3. Wash inside of egg shell thoroughly with water and a little white vinegar. Allow to dry completely.

4. Shape small indent in centre of oasis. Apply a small quantity of glue to indent and position egg at angle required. Allow glue to dry.

5. In a small bowl break up green dried flowers into small pieces. Using finger tips spread a thick covering of glue on outside of shell. Quickly press green flowers into glue on outside of egg. Allow glue to dry.

6. Break stalks off bright yellow daisies. Working from inside back apply small quantity of glue. Using tweezers position flower heads. Continue until entire inside is covered. Allow to dry.

7. Break heads off white daisies and glue in circle around edge of opening. Allow glue to dry.

8. Break stems off yellow and white flowers leaving approx. 1 cm (⅜") stem attached to flower head. Carefully push flower heads into foam until all the surface is covered.

9. Spray with clear lacquer to seal. Allow to thoroughly dry.

10. Apply thin covering of glue around edge of foam. Position yellow satin ribbon around edge of foam taking care to secure join at rear of arrangement. Allow to dry.

11. Tie bow in cord and glue in position in front of egg. Allow to dry.

12. When egg is completely dry place chicken in egg.

ADDITIONAL IDEAS

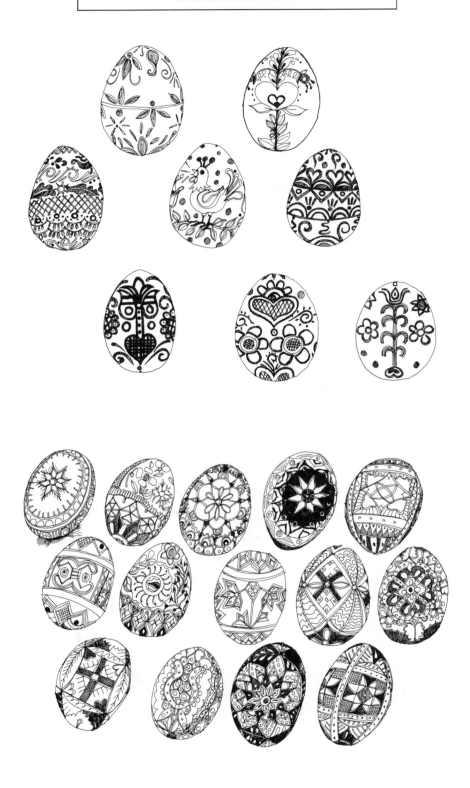

Other books by the same author:

'Patonga' Country Kitchen
The Explorer's Country Kitchen
Wheat-Free Cooking
Milk-Free Cooking
Low-Sugar Cooking for those with Diabetes